AF441198

OPTIMIZED OUTCOMES

Financial Solutions to Help You Make the Most of Your Future

Vijay Khetarpal, AIF®, CLU®, ChFC®, CFP®

Foreword by Kawaljit S. Bhutani, MBA, CPA

"We help protect your tomorrows"

The author will contribute the profits from the sale of this book to Nonprofit Foundations that do work to improve the lives of those less fortunate, including but not limited to Rotary International and the Million Dollar Round Table Foundation.

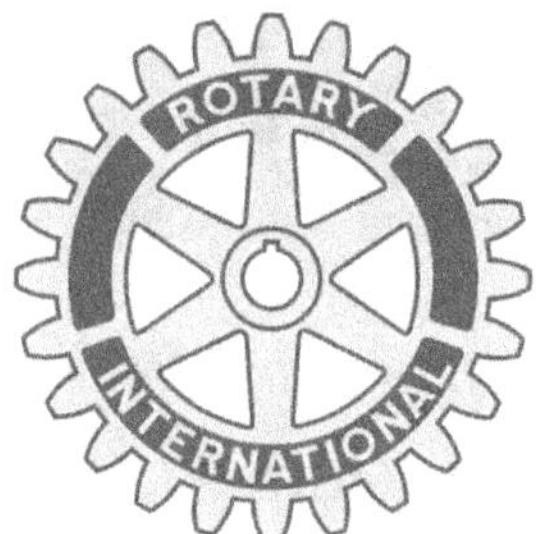

Copyright © 2020 by Vijay Khetarpal. All rights reserved.
ISBN: 9798694954617

Integrity Financial Group, LLC, does not offer legal or tax advice. Please consult the appropriate professional regarding your individual circumstance.

Not associated with or endorsed by the Social Security Administration or any other government agency.

Securities and advisory services offered through Royal Alliance Associates, Inc. (RAA), member FINRA/SIPC. RAA is separately owned and other entities and/or marketing names, products or services referenced here are independent of RAA.

Qualifying membership in the MDRT is based on minimum commission and gross business generated within a year. Each MDRT status designation is granted for one year only. All members must apply every year to continue their affiliation with the Million Dollar Round Table.

Dedication

This book is dedicated with immense love to my wife, Anila, who has always believed in me, has patiently tolerated me for many years, and does much to take care of my life and health while I focus on business pursuits and my passion for golf and travel. Somehow, she has been able to manage the twin tasks of being simultaneously my strongest critic yet my most ardent defender, which is much valued to make me a better person every passing day. For that, I am grateful beyond words.

It is my hope that the ideas shared here will be beneficial to our future generations and to the readers and their extended families and businesses.

Table of Contents

Acknowledgments

I want to thank the following people, each of whom has made a positive impact on my career and life in some way. Thank you for your inspiration, guidance, and example.

- Guy Baker
- Ben Baldwin
- Alex Baqir
- Glen Blauch
- Daryl Brockman
- Stephen Covey
- Frank DellaPenna
- Bruce Etherington
- Mehdi Fakharzadeh
- Sidney Friedman
- Joe Gandolfo
- Rao Garuda
- Bill Haraway
- Tom Hegna
- John Huggard
- Kevin Hutto
- Joe Jordan
- Barry Kaye
- Don Lawson
- David McKnight
- Irwin Burt Meisel
- Moshe Milevsky
- Nick Murray
- Steve Parrish
- Wade Pfau
- Steve Plewes
- James Ruth
- John Savage
- Randy Scritchfield
- Simon Singer
- Ed Slott, CPA
- Dan Sullivan
- Atul Thakkar
- Brian Tracy
- Dick Webber
- Howard Wight
- Thomas Wolff
- Roger Zener
- Zig Ziglar

In the Recommended Reading section at the back of this book are selected titles of books and other resources that some of these knowledgeable people have written.

Foreword

As the saying goes, there are two definites in life: death and taxes. I would argue that the there is more in common to each of these than just being a mandatory part of life. One needs to plan for each, as not planning for them can cause serious misfortune. Each of us has come across clients who did not plan for either and suffered major financial consequences.

Vijay and I met at a conference several years ago. We hit it off and have been friends and business associates ever since. Although we each own our independent businesses, he and I collaborate on many matters and now share many mutual clients. We each work with clients from all walks of life—varying incomes, ages, careers, etc.

No matter your background, one of the most important aspects of your life is your money. Money is something that everyone wants and needs. For most people, there is never enough money. Someone making $50,000 looks forward to the time when he or she makes $100,000. The person making $100,000 now wants to make $250,000. Millionaires are striving to become billionaires. For most people, no matter what income level they are at, it is never enough.

When you hear the term "living paycheck to paycheck," you normally would picture an hourly wage employee who is trying to figure out how to make enough for next month's rent. I thought the same way until I started preparing individual tax returns. In 1994, I was twenty-three years old when I started working part-time at H&R Block. I was making $10/hour and was very happy because my previous job paid only $9/hour.

While it was a job, it was also an education for me. At that time, I was still unsure if I had chosen the correct field. I had recently graduated with an accounting degree and was studying for the CPA exam. The job and H&R Block gave me a window into people's finances, and I learned how much various careers paid. As a tax accountant, you get insight into one of clients' deepest secrets— their money.

I came across people from all professions and saw what they made. We had bus drivers, butchers, government employees, athletes, scientists, and others. It was a fascinating experience and the best financial education one could ever have. I learned more about money in those tax seasons than I did in four years of college, and even subsequently business school.

In particular, I came across a client who was the basis of my education. Her name was Alice. She had earned her PhD in biology and was earning more than $100,000 as a research director. Remember, this was 1994…it was rare to see someone making $100,000. While she had a large amount of earned income, her bank interest income was less than $10. That would imply that her savings totaled less than $5,000.

I was amazed that someone making in excess of $100,000 could not save more than $5,000. As her income increased over the years, so did her expenses. Maybe she could not control some of those expenses, but there were definitely some she could have controlled—the car she drove, the home she lived in, the clothes she wore, etc. Typically, after our tax appointment, she would show me her new car and tell me about the stuff she had bought. In my final year at that office, things were different. She had lost her job, and that caused her to lose her home to foreclosure. She had to return her new car. All she was left with was a bunch of nice clothes, but no job to wear them to.

Her experience reminded me of a lesson my father had given to me about money. One day he told me, "Son, there are only two ways to have more money in the bank. Either you make more, or you spend less." I live by that today. Think for a moment how simple that concept is.

In addition to reminding me about an important life lesson, it also dawned on me how there was never a class in college that taught us how to manage our money. We are always taught how to make ourselves more valuable to our future employers so they will pay us more—but never how to intelligently manage it. I asked around to friends and colleagues about this "revelation" I had. Each one told me the same thing: they learned how to manage their money on the fly. On-the-job training, so to speak. Alice may have benefited from such a class.

After several jobs, and getting my MBA, I finally opened my own tax accounting practice in 2011. Along the way, I was always interested in learning about all aspects of personal finance. I wanted to know about everything—taxes, loans, investing, savings, insurance. I have always made it a point to network with individuals in similar fields: wealth managers, insurance agents, loan officers, bankers, attorneys, and anyone else in complimentary fields. Many of these folks have become good friends and contacts. In addition to those network connections helping me out in my business, those professionals have been a source for a wealth of information that would make me a better resource to my clients.

As I started working with my own clients, I noticed that many were like the aforementioned Alice. They were all missing one thing: planning. We have navigation systems to get from here to there. We use recipe cards when we are baking a cake or preparing a meal. We pick our clothes to create an outfit. Each of these is an example of planning. If we are planning what we are going to cook, then why are we all not planning how we are going to manage our money? That may be the most important plan of all. The meal is over in a couple of hours, but the financial plan will last us our entire adult lives. In my profession, I work with my clients on tax planning. But there are many other aspects to planning—college, debt, retirement, and yes... even death.

Planning is difficult. The reason is that plans are specific to each person. There are only so many ways to make pumpkin pie, and there are only so many ways to get home from work. But there are thousands of variables to a financial plan. Your income, your spending, your goals, your family, your job, your health…everything. This plan is akin to a long journey that lasts your whole life, and it should be able to adapt to a change in each variable.

The purpose of this book is to offer you education so that you can begin the preparation of your financial plan. Vijay gives you guidelines and tips on how to manage your finances. He goes over investments, life insurance, taxes, investing, saving, retirement, and so much more. Each chapter will force you to think about your financial situation. The lessons in this book apply to every single one of us, no matter your age, profession, income profile, or financial background. While the lessons apply to each of us, your financial plan will be different than the one for person next to you.

The hope is you will be able to start understanding your finances and be able to develop your own financial plan. But it does not end there. The key to any plan is to stick to it. You will need key advisors whom you can meet with who will work with you on keeping yourself to your plan. Of course there will be deviations—a detour here, a bridge closed there. However, you need to keep the spirit of the plan intact.

In this book, Vijay covers many different topics and offers you many strategies/ideas. There may be terms and concepts that are not yet familiar to you yet. Write those down so you can look them up later. Then you should decide which of these are of interest to you. If you need to, then find advisors whom you can trust and help you in your planning exercise.

I was never able to keep in touch with Alice, as I moved out of the area from where that H&R Block office was located. However, I hope she finds this book.

Happy reading! Happy planning!

Kawaljit S. Bhutani, MBA, CPA

Introduction: My Story

As a financial advisor for almost four decades, I am committed—along with my highly competent, knowledgeable, and compassionate team—to partnering with my clients to help optimize their outcomes. I like to focus on solutions. In this book, I have outlined strategies that I hope will help you optimize your own financial and personal outcomes.

Before we jump into the details about financial planning, however, I want to share my own story with you. Hopefully, by sharing with you a little about myself and why should you care to hear me will be helpful to the cause. As I share with you some struggles I have overcome, you will see why I have devoted my life's work to helping others find suitable financial strategies and make the most of what they have.

I Did Not Let a Congenital Condition Define Me

I was born two months premature in 1958. I was in the hospital for the first three weeks of my life because in the India of the 1950s, the survival rate for premature babies was pretty low. The doctors wanted to keep a close eye on me. My godmother, Kamala, took care of me while my mother was in recovery. Fortunately for me, I was able to survive that ordeal and, till, this day believe myself to be a member of the Lucky Sperm Club.

My development was somewhat delayed. Also, I did not realize it because I didn't know any different, but for the first several years of my life, I had a hearing loss since birth.

I did not know that I couldn't hear properly; I just thought I heard what I heard. When I had to ask someone to repeat what they said, I just thought it was because they didn't speak loudly enough, or they were not speaking to me. In other words, I didn't know what I didn't know, which is that I could not hear well. My loss of hearing was not across all frequencies; it was only at certain frequencies. So I could hear some sounds perfectly, like any normal person, but I could not hear some sounds at all. Over time, I learned to read people's lips so I could understand what they were saying.

During my early years in school, because I couldn't hear properly, I wasn't able to learn as fast as the other children. As a student, I was not particularly comfortable, nor was I particularly successful. A lot of times, because I did not hear sounds properly, I would speak words the way I heard them, and I couldn't understand why my communication was not getting through. What you speak is based on what you hear. And I did not even know that I was missing that connection. Some of my classmates even made fun of my muffled speech.

When I was about fifteen years old, one of the teachers told my parents that I needed to be tested, so my parents took me to have a hearing test. That is when they got the confirmation about my hearing loss. Back then, the technology for improving hearing was not as advanced as it is today. Essentially, they gave me a loudspeaker that was about the size of a Sony Walkman. I carried it with me, and it amplified all sounds—even those sounds I could hear perfectly fine. So the sounds I could hear well before became very loud—too loud. And the sounds I had not been able to hear before sounded very strange to me; I didn't know what those sounds were. I never really adapted to that technology.

One of the best decisions my parents made for me, in terms of education, was to put me in a boarding school. My father was in the Indian Air Force and was reassigned to a new post every few years. If I had moved with them, my schooling would have suffered.

At age nine, I took a boarding school entrance exam which I failed. In retrospect, I am glad I failed because it would have landed me in a different boarding school with perhaps a very different experience. Thanks to my parents' commitment and encouragement for a very healthy self-esteem from early childhood, I was not in any way disheartened when I failed. At age ten, I took the entrance exam again and ended up getting into Mayo College Ajmer.

Mayo College is a boys' residential public school in Ajmer, Rajasthan, India. It was founded in 1875 by Richard Bourke, the 6th Earl of Mayo, who was also the Viceroy of India from 1869 to 1872. The school is one of the oldest public boarding schools of India.[1]

The boarding school had an excellent sports infrastructure, and several different sports were played simultaneously. That is what paved the way for my strong sportsman's spirit. At Mayo, I formed enduring bonds with friends that last till this day. Also, I was able to excel beyond academics and focus on becoming a well-rounded person. I participated in aquatics and swam at the Rajasthan state level.

I was keenly aware of the sacrifices my family made to afford me this boarding school opportunity, on an Indian Air Force officer's meager salary. My parents' love and teacher's encouragement fed my determination to not let my congenital hearing loss define me or prevent me from succeeding. I even served as the School Monitor in my senior year.

Despite my hearing loss, I graduated from high school—not only second in my class, but also, I was ranked fourteenth among the entire population of graduating seniors in the whole country. In India, about 15,000 of us took the All India Higher Secondary exam in 1975. I wasn't expected to do well, but when it mattered most, I was able to succeed. As my wife, Anila, likes to say, under pressure, I perform.

To finish high school at the top 0.001 percent of my fellow graduates, despite my hearing loss, shows what you can accomplish when you are determined. I have always believed that there is no bigger disability than a bad attitude. If your attitude is good, all obstacles come to instruct, not obstruct. I am grateful that in my early childhood, I cultivated a healthy attitude toward all things in life.

At Mayo, along with swimming, I took up squash as a sport. The sport of squash was invented in a prison. I loved it because I could play it on my own, using the walls. In addition to my good grades, my sports excellence helped me gain admission into St. Stephen's College, the oldest (est. 1881) and best college, now part of the Delhi University in Delhi, India.

I continued to play squash at the national level. It is quite a demanding sport, both physically and mentally. At one point, my only goal in life was to be a top-level squash player, perhaps even turn professional, and teach the game to others.

In college, I was pretty independent. By then, my father had retired from the Indian Air Force, and my family had settled in Delhi. Even then, my parents afforded me an opportunity to live on campus, though it was not customary for the students who lived in town to do so. Playing competitive squash afforded me opportunities to travel to other parts of the country and play with various players. Living on campus definitely enhanced my bonds with my batchmates, as well as my squash contemporaries.

Thanks to my experiences at Mayo and St. Stephen's College, I formed friendships that sustain me till this day. I graduated with a bachelor's degree in economics, with honors.

Off to Nigeria and Then the United States

When I graduated from college in 1978, I went to Nigeria to work. In 1971, Nigeria had joined the Organization of Petroleum Exporting Countries (OPEC) to contribute to decisions on global energy demand and supply issues with the other OPEC member countries.

Because Nigeria was a major oil producer, the country was attractive in potential income opportunities for young people who were just starting their careers, certainly in terms of Indian currency. At that time, one Naira was equal to $1.70.

While working in Nigeria, I visited the United States several times, and life brought me to the United States in 1983 for good. I remember that $1 was equal to 7.80 Indian Rupees (INR), and now $1 is equal to approximately INR 78; I would say we have experienced considerable devaluation of the Rupee to the Dollar.

At that time, I did not want to work for someone else because no company would pay me the kind of income that I was used to earning as an expatriate in Nigeria. I didn't want to cut my income, and I was willing to pay the price for success—essentially the price everyone pays, either before success or after failure.

I thought, "No disrespect, but instead of working for a bank or any other company on a salary, I want to build my own business." Though I did not have any capital to invest, I did have a background in Economics and Finance. I decided to get into the insurance business to learn the ropes, which paved the way to my Financial advisory business.

Launching My Insurance Career at New York Life

In late 1983, I decided to start on the insurance side of the business because everyone needs insurance—protection—whether or not they understand or realize the value of it. My thinking was that most people need insurance, whereas not everybody has money to invest. I started working with New York Life. My managers, Alex Baqir and Frank DellaPenna, taught me the business. I've got to compliment them—it's a good company, especially when you are just getting started. Their wonderful training programs offered a fertile ground for someone like me: young, ambitious, and willing to work hard. I must credit my winning attitude again to my upbringing and encouraging sports career.

After starting out in life insurance sales, I was named Rookie of the Year and soon became a top producer for a couple of consecutive years at my office in Silver Spring, Maryland. Then I was asked to replicate my habits and my strategies, attract other people into the business, and mentor them as a Sales Manager. I got into the recruiting game on behalf of New York Life and did that for a few years. As a matter of fact, that is how I met my wife, Anila.

In the early 1990s, I realized that I had enjoyed solving problems for my clients far more than recruiting or managing other producers. Till this day, I take pride in helping my individual and corporate clients understand the power of life insurance and its many creative uses and help design solutions for pennies on the dollar.

Around that time, I completed my Certified Financial Planner™ (CFP®) designation. According to the CFP Board's code of ethics, you have to be independent to be a CFP. This made perfect sense to me because, regardless of how expansive a company is, no single company can possibly have every solution to every client's needs, all the time, in a cost-effective fashion. Independent advisors, on the other hand, can provide suitable solutions from many different companies, which provides clients with a vast array of options. That scenario appealed to me a lot because I have always been focused on finding appropriate strategies for my clients.

At the end of 1995, I made the decision to leave New York Life and strike out on my own. I became a personal producer as well as a recruiter. That's where I learned my next lesson.

I became a General Agent for John Hancock Life Insurance Company. I lasted for about three years in the agency ownership role, but I was not having fun. Once again, I was spending too much time managing the business and the people and too little time managing client relationships, which was—and is—the most important aspect of the business to me till this day. They say experience is never wasted; you always learn. That is true. Even though I was not happy at John Hancock as a General Agent, I continued to establish my connections and increase my knowledge of the insurance industry.

In 1999, Integrity Financial Group was formed, and I've been an independent producer ever since then. The only people I answer to are my clients. I don't work for any company, and I am not beholden to any strategy or product. Our team's only goal is to optimize outcomes for our clients.

During my thirty-seven years in business, I have experienced all kinds of ups and downs. I've seen people and products come and go from this industry. I've served clients through many life events such as marriage, childbirth, business formation, bankruptcy, divorce, premature death, premature disability, long-term nursing-care costs, and business mistakes. I've known people who thought they would return to their home country when they retired but didn't because their kids and grandkids are here. Serving my clients through a lot of situations, upheavals, and uncertainties has made me a better advisor. I'm able to take the teachings of experiences from one client's situation, obviously without jeopardizing any confidential information, and apply the lessons learned therein with another client who might have had the same outcome but was able to fare much better because of the knowledge my team and I had gained and were able to share.

An Important Life Lesson

Having been through a divorce and other business failures myself, I have learned an important life lesson: to stick with what I know.

In early 2000, I invested in a restaurant franchise and set out to open several restaurants around the area. It's a business that looks very mundane and relatively easy as an investor. Everybody eats out, right? But we quickly learned that it is actually a very difficult and demanding business. Though we operated for a few years, the effort became a significant cash drain. In a situation like that, eventually you have to cut your losses. After a few years of struggling to make it work, it had to be shut down and written off.

The lesson I learned there is that it's better to stick to your core competency. You can't be all things to all people. Yes, you can diversify a little bit—but do it in areas related to your specialty. Today, in addition to handling our clients' life, health, disability, and long-term care insurance needs, we also manage investments, 401(k) plans, defined benefit plans, IRAs, employee benefits, and other products. In short, we are providing comprehensive financial-advisory and wealth-management services to businesses and families.

These areas are all connected. But there is really no connection between a restaurant business and a financial advisory business. I made a renewed commitment to my core business.

I think it is wise not to stray too far from your core competency.

Everyone Needs a Coach

I realized that, as a business owner, the positive side was that I was not answerable to anybody., I enjoyed a lot of independence. But the negative side was that I had no sounding board as I had when I worked for a company. I needed somebody who would tell me what I *needed* to hear, not what I *liked* to hear.

Every Olympian or exceptional athlete you can think of—including Tiger Woods, Tom Brady, and Michael Jordan—have coaches, even when they are at the top of their game.

I had heard a lot of good things about Coach Dan Sullivan and his program called The Strategic Coach®, so I signed up for the three-year program. It was an investment in myself and quite intensive. After about a year of doing all the work and traveling to Chicago every quarter, I was getting frustrated because I was spending a lot of money with the coach, but I was not seeing any results.

One day, I remarked to my coach, "Dan, you just figured out a way to increase my overhead, but I'm not seeing any results."

He said, "Remember, you signed up for a three-year program. Are we into the third year yet?"

I said, "No."

"Just keep it up," he advised. "Do what you have to do, and you will see the difference."

Boy, was he right! After another year, I suddenly started to notice the difference. That coaching program has been highly instrumental in how my team and I operate our business today—with our clients, our business, our free time, and our resources. Honestly, if not for that program, we probably would not be doing business the way we do it today. I cannot say enough good things about The Strategic Coach.

No one person has a patent on all the good ideas in or for any business. It is important that you not only work *in* your business, but that you also work *on* your business. Now I am constantly looking at ways to enhance not only the outcomes for our clients, but equally important, to enhance the way we do our business in a way that benefits our clients and our team.

Today, I take a lot of pride in being a mentor and an educator at heart to everyone we meet, including our clients, prospects, other advisors, and allied professionals. They say that teachers often learn more from teaching than the students themselves. I believe that is true.

Modeling Work–Life Balance for Our Clients

One day, someone asked me, "How long will you keep doing this?"

I replied, "I enjoy my business and serving my clients. I don't see myself completely retiring from it ever—at least not any time soon."

One strategy that will enable me to continue working as long as I wish is that I take the time to create a good balance in my life. Anila and I love to travel a lot and spend time with our beautifully blended family. We have three boys, two wonderful daughters-in-law, a two-year-old grandson who is an absolute joy, and a brand-new granddaughter.

In addition to serving our clients, I enjoy playing golf and my Rotary service. Those are my top priorities. Fortunately, I am blessed with a good team at work, a strong support system at home, and technology that enables me to enjoy this balance.

As I apply effective strategies to my own life, I also share them with my clients. I strive to help them optimize their outcomes, not only in terms of financial confidence and strength, but also in terms of taking the time to enjoy their lives along the way. We all live one heartbeat at a time; there are no guarantees in life—something we all recently learned from COVID-19 pretty much stopping everything in its tracks. Regardless of our age or net worth, we have all been touched by this storm. By sharing our experiences with the children and grandchildren of our clients, we strive to learn and grow from this situation and to minimize its impact on our finances and well-being.

My golf handicap is still a little higher than I would like, but overall, Anila and I love the situation we are in. We have a lot of gratitude for our clients and feel blessed with the business, our life together, and our good health.

I am also grateful for the support I have received throughout my life. The blessings I now enjoy could not have happened without my parents and teachers being the beacon of light in my early life. And today, I am incredibly fortunate to have the support I receive from my staff, my clients, and my wife. If I had to do it all over again, I may not wish to change much.

> **Each one of our so-called "failures" teaches us something that propels us to a greater degree of success.**

How we look at things—our perspective—is important. Some people look at a glass half-empty, and some people look at the same glass and consider it half-full. I prefer to be the eternal optimist. A positive attitude may not let us do everything, but it will let us do anything better than a negative attitude will.

Even though hope is not a strategy, my approach is to plan for the worst and hope for the best. I sleep peacefully every night, despite all the noise in the market.

I hope you can identify with at least a part of my story. Even if one idea in this book will help you navigate the noise in your life, in your career, and in the market, I would consider it a mission accomplished. We all learn from the difficulties we endure; they can make us better and stronger individuals than we ever thought ourselves to be capable of. Although I may not be able to help you avoid obstacles in your life, I do hope to help you navigate them with ease and learn, along with you, some of the valuable lessons they present. I hope the strategies in this book will help you do just that.

About This Book

This is a story about preparing for the future, and I believe that both consumers/investors and financial advisors will benefit from it. At Integrity Financial Group, my team and I specialize in building financial plans for clients based on strategies for various generations, as well as for small, closely held businesses and nonprofits. We serve many people who have investible assets exceeding $1 million; pre-retirees ages fifty to seventy; younger professionals in high-paying white-collar positions such as doctors, IT consultants, engineers and lawyers as well as small-business owners.

Whatever your situation is, the key is to be prepared and to plan for the future. The coronavirus, or COVID-19, pandemic has thrust a lot of people into financial hardship because they didn't plan for a disruption in their income. Yet if history is a guide; every crisis presents plenty of opportunities to be seized.

This book is intended to educate you about financial topics. However, to truly optimize your financial outcome, we recommend that you work with a highly competent, trustworthy financial advisor to navigate the complex world of financial planning and get your financial house in order. An experienced, independent, credentialed financial advisor who adheres to the fiduciary standard (always acting in the best interest of the client) is worth his or her fees in gold.

It is critical that you work with a financial advisor who will develop a financial plan that is thoughtfully tailored to your unique needs, dreams, and financial situation. Advisors who provide financial plans built from templates, without getting to know you as a unique individual, are doing a huge disservice. Be wary of any advisor who begins offering you products or services without fully understanding your situation and goals.

A Rx without a diagnosis is malpractice.

The overwhelming majority of our clients have had some level of planning done previously. Regardless of all the good work done in the past by their advisors, our clients find it worthwhile to get a fresh opinion through another set of eyes. The biggest omission we see during these reviews is the lack of a periodic review or document audit. Because financial planning and each client's unique needs are dynamic, and no one person or firm has a patent on all the good ideas in the business; often we are able to add significant value by capturing opportunities and closing any gaps in our clients' strategies to optimize their outcomes.

I wrote this book because I feel there is a dearth of written material about these important strategies and how to implement them. I hope these strategies and solutions, based on my almost forty-year career as a financial advisor, will help you optimize *your* outcomes.

CHAPTER 1

Money Comes, Money Goes

People often ask me what percentage of their income they should spend on their mortgage, savings, and other expenses.

I have several guidelines that can help people establish a budget and set financial goals for themselves. Having a budget can help you manage cash flow, which is an important aspect of planning for the future.

Most people have no idea where their money goes. When you develop a budget and get into the habit of following it closely, it makes you more aware of your spending habits. It also helps you make better choices so you can save more money for the future and be prepared when emergencies come up.

> Systematize the predictable so you can humanize the unexpected.

I developed the following family cash-flow diagram to help families see a visual representation of suggested allotments of funds in specific areas.

Family Cash-Flow Diagram

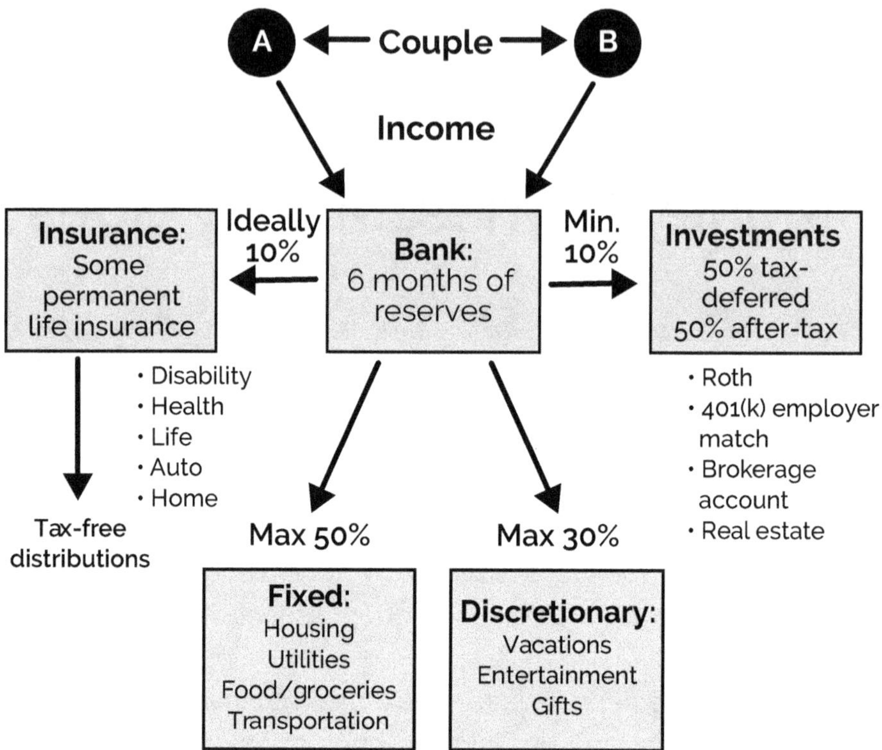

Notes:

1. During your healthy/young years, work for your money. During your later/retirement years, your money works for you.
2. If your investments do well, insurance becomes a smaller part of your net worth. If your investments do poorly, insurance provides emergency relief. In the event of premature death or disability, insurance completes your plan.

The 50–30–20 Rule

To balance spending and saving, I call my general rule the "50–30–20" rule. Some people call it the "20–30–50 rule." It has become a popular rule of thumb since Senator Elizabeth Warren and her daughter have discussed it in public. Here is the breakdown:

- **50**: You should anticipate spending about 50 percent of your income—half of it—on necessities. That includes housing, food, and utilities.
- **30**: I recommend spending approximately 30 percent of your income on discretionary expenses, such as clothing, upgrading to a newer vehicle model, and splurging on a vacation. This category also includes smaller indulgences like going to see a movie, eating dinner out, and other entertainment—having fun.
- **20**: I recommend spending the remaining 20 percent of your income on savings, investments, and debt reduction.

Some people like to change the categories a little and use ranges instead of set percentages. For example, I've had clients budget 25 to 35 percent of their income for housing, 10 to 15 percent for food, 5 to 10 percent for utilities, 10 percent for transportation, 10 percent for all types of insurance, 10 to 20 percent for savings, 10 to 15 percent for fun/entertainment, 5 to 10 percent for personal expenses, and any income that's left over for a miscellaneous category, to include anything that's not listed in the other categories.

It is fine to adjust these percentages in a way that works for you. The important thing is to manage your cash flow by budgeting. If you do that, you will have an excellent start to planning for the future. Adhering to your budget on a regular basis probably won't happen overnight; it is a process.

You might be surprised to learn that your largest single expense category is not be a home mortgage or your children's education; almost always, it is taxes. So clearly, managing those properly will help you optimize other allocations.

Our Spending Habits Change with Age

We spend money differently in different stages of life. For most Americans on average the expenses increase annually until they are in their 50's. However, as the following chart shows how we spend less on some types of expenses as we age and more on others. You will also notice that the average American's total expenditures decrease with age as well.

Annual Spending	Age 55–64 $55,892	Age 65–74 $46,757	Age 75+ $34,382	% Change 55–75+
Apparel & Services	$1,563	$1,222	$768	–51%
Entertainment	2,651	2,488	1,422	–46%
Food & Alcohol	7,176	6,420	4,376	–39%
Health Care	4,378	5,188	4,910	+12%
Housing	17,937	15,639	12,314	–31%
Transportation	9,482	7,972	5,149	–46%
Miscellaneous & Other	5,672	4,436	4,375	–23%
Personal Insurance & Other	7,033	3,392	1,068	–85%
Total Expenditures	**$55,892**	**$46,757**	**$34,382**	**–38%**

Source: US Department of Labor, Bureau of Labor Statistics, Consumer Expenditure Survey, September 2014

How Much to Keep in "Liquid" Assets

I noted earlier that I recommend earmarking approximately 20 percent of your income for savings, investments, and debt reduction.

Getting more specific, we like our clients to, ideally, maintain a minimum of six months' worth of expenses in reserves and liquid assets. For example, if a household is operating on $10,000 per month, then they should have, ideally, about $60,000 in cash or cash equivalents. These funds need not be in a checking account. They can be in a savings account, a money market account, or any other investment that is "liquid," or easily accessible. Additionally, ROTH IRA contributions and cash value life insurance are good proxies for emergency funds as well.

> **Build up an emergency fund that's equal to at least six months' worth of expenses.**

Some people tend to be much more conservative than that. For example, sometimes, older people want to maintain more money in liquid assets. People who own businesses with cyclical and unpredictable cycles often set aside more money in liquid assets. Someone who is the only income earner in the family might do the same.

On the other hand, some people tend to abide by less conservative guidelines. For example, people who have good job security and wants to take a greater degree of risk might keep less money in liquid assets and invest more in stocks, in the hopes of getting a good return—growth—on that money. Because they have security in their jobs, they have a source of stable income and can take more risks with investment dollars. Whatever the reason might be, sometimes people dial their liquid assets down as situations tend to be dynamic.

Mortgage Guidelines

When people are looking to buy a new home or refinance their current mortgage, they want to know how much home they can afford to buy. Often, people ask me this question when they are planning to get married.

The guideline I share is that an outstanding mortgage—not your mortgage payment—should not exceed 3 to 3.5 times your annual income. Let's say your annual salary is $100,000. Ideally, you want to keep your outstanding mortgage balance at about $300,000. Now, that doesn't mean you have to buy a house that's worth $300,000. Typically, when you buy a house, you make a down payment. So, if you were going to put $100,000 down on the mortgage, then with your $100,000 annual salary, you could probably buy a house of about $400,000.

Again, someone who is more conservative might use the guideline of 2.5 times his or her annual salary. And someone who is comfortable with more risk might use 3.5 times the annual salary as a guideline for an outstanding mortgage. Ideally, it should be who will take more risks, then it can go up to three and a half times.

Investment Guidelines

Another guideline people often ask for is how much money they should put in investments such as stocks and bonds.

Again, this is a function of many variables, but a starting point is to subtract your age from 120, and that is an ideal percentage of assets to invest in Equities. For example, if you are 50 years of age, then 120 minus 50 is 70; approximately 70 percent of your assets should be in the equity markets and similar investments.

Now, if someone is only 30 years of age, then 120 minus 30 is 90. That person should ideally invest 90 percent of his or her assets in the stock market.

Guidelines for Retirement Savings

Another question people often ask is, "How much money do I need to retire?" Again, many factors affect this number, including your time horizon (how many years before you retire), where you want to live in retirement, whether or not you plan to keep working when you retire, and if you will still be paying a mortgage when you retire.

We do not advise people to focus only on their total amount of assets. Instead, we want them to focus on how much *guaranteed lifelong income* they can get. But again, we do offer a guideline to help people plan. We advise that you should plan to have a minimum of 20 times your annual income once you retire. Again, a more conservative person might shoot for 25 times his or her income, and a less conservative person might shoot for 15 times his or her annual salary. (We also use the Income Stability Ratio, which is, in effect, this formula: Stable income ÷ Needed income = Income stability ratio.)

If your annual income is $100,000, and that is the amount of money your lifestyle is based on, then your target for retirement savings should be 20 X $100,000, which is $2 million. If you live on 5 percent of your retirement savings per year, 5 percent of $2 million is $100,000. That gives you the same level of income in retirement that you have grown accustomed to during your earning years.

You can do this calculation in reverse, too. (If a person who is age 65 has $500,000 worth of investments, he or she should assume income of $25,000—simply divide 500 by 20.

Your Ideal Net Worth at a Certain Age

Another question that comes up from some people is, "How am I doing for my age?" People like to compare where they are on their financial journey with other people in their age group. In my view, this doesn't matter, but some people like to have a benchmark to see how they're doing.

Your net worth is, essentially, your assets minus your liabilities. A guideline we use is that your ideal net worth should be your current age times your pretax annual income, divided by 10. Let's say you are 30 years old and, again, your income is $100,000 per year:

30 X $100,000 = $3 million, and $3 million ÷ 10 = $300,000

According to this guideline, at age 30, you should ideally have approximately $300,000 worth of assets, including home equity, your bank account, and investments. If your net worth isn't quite at the number this guideline suggests, then you have some catching up to do. If you are ahead of that number, then you are doing well.

The Present Value of Social Security Income should be included unless, of course, you are in the group of people who don't believe Social Security will be there for you once you retire.

Guidelines for Life Insurance Coverage

One more question people ask a lot is, "How much life insurance should I have?" As a guideline, we have found that 10 times your annual income is a good starting point. If your annual salary is $100,000, then 10 X $100,000 = $1 million. You need, at a minimum, $1 million in life insurance coverage.

This had nothing to do with how much life insurance coverage you have through your employer. It is a matter of the total death benefit your family will receive when you pass away.

Life insurance protects your future, your tomorrows. You need sufficient life insurance coverage to replace your income for your surviving family members. A good way to realize the importance of sufficient life insurance coverage is to ask yourself the following questions:

How Much Are Your Tomorrows Worth?

<table>
<tr>
<td>If you had been killed in a car accident last week and someone else had been responsible for your death, how much would your family be suing for?

$_____________</td>
<td>How much life insurance do you have?

$_____________</td>
</tr>
</table>

Now, how do those two numbers match up?

Figure Out Your Current Level of Spending

When we work with our clients to establish budgets, we start out by getting an idea of their current spending. We will review the last three months' or six months' worth of expenses from bank statements and credit-card statements. That is a good starting point for anyone in establishing a budget.

Keep in mind that these guidelines and numbers will change over time. Your financial situation is always changing.

The ratio we start out with isn't likely to be the same one we end up with two decades later. People's life situations change. They get married, buy homes, have children, send children to college, start businesses, and retire.

Of course the numbers I have discussed in this chapter will differ according to your level of income and where you live. Also, these guidelines would need to be adjusted if your income is based on commission. And sometimes, we make adjustments for couples with dual incomes.

I cannot stress enough that these are just guidelines. As with any aspect of financial planning, it is imperative that you work with a qualified financial advisor to go over your specific financial situation and establish a plan based on your unique needs and goals.

Chapter 1 Call to Action:

Review three to six months of past expenditures in your bank account and credit card accounts to determine how much you generally spend each month and year and in which categories. Then, using the guidelines in chapter 1, develop a budget for your family and/or business. Anticipate spending approximately 50 percent of your income on necessities, 30 percent on discretionary expenses, and 20 percent on savings, investments, and debt reduction.

The Swiss Army Knife of Financial Planning

> **The skillful use of life insurance can improve almost any financial transaction.**

What if you could grow your money tax-free; access up to 90 percent of your money at any time tax-free; get most of the gains of the market; never participate in the losses; and, when you pass it on to your heirs, it doubles, triples, or more tax-free? Would that be of interest to you?

Most people would say yes. And the way you can accomplish all that is to leverage life insurance to optimize future outcomes.

Many affluent people include life insurance as an integral part of their portfolios. This is because they understand the economics of monetary efficiency, leverage, hedging, and legacy-creation capabilities with "other people's money," as opposed to using their own 100 cent-dollars. Here are some examples of situations that call for the use of life insurance by the wealthy:

- To fund the payment of estate taxes with discounted dollars
- To create additional liquidity so valuable family assets do not have to be sold
- To create estate equalization among heirs, particularly when

some specific assets (such as a business) are not going to be shared equally
- To develop key-person and business continuity indemnification
- To provide charitable bequests or replace the wealth left by family to charity or provide for perpetual giving to charity
- To provide for children from multiple marriages
- To recapture taxes paid for distributions from retirement plans or other post-mortem taxes
- To leverage assets already in trusts

Did You Know You Can Finance Your Life Insurance Premium?

Sometimes—either because the need for life insurance far exceeds a person's cash flow available for premiums or because of attractive financing and leverage—you can consider premium financing arrangements from banks.

Premium Finance Strategy Design

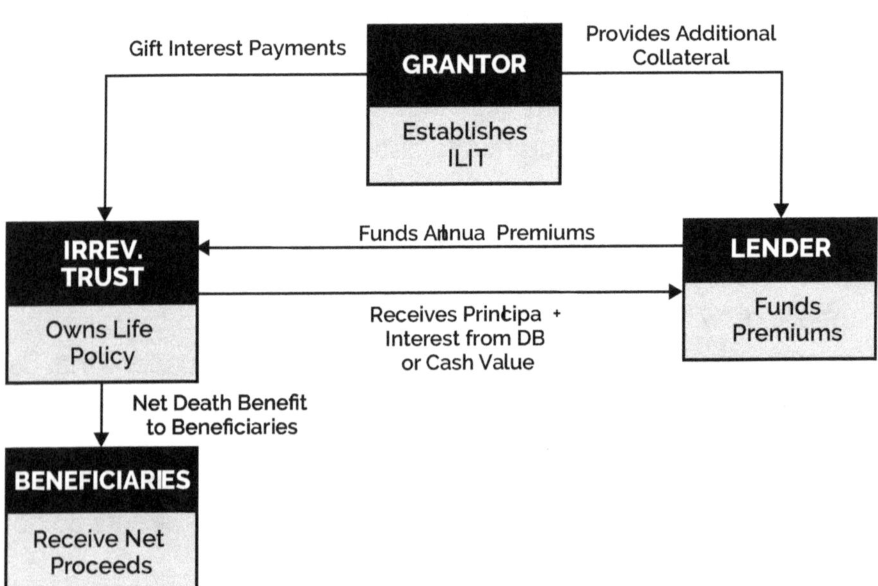

For most premium financing cases; the net worth of the individual or family needs to be at least $5 million with annual premiums of $100,000. Typically the client pays the interest on the loans, whereas the bank provides low-interest-rate financing for a specified number of years, with the policy as collateral. Sometimes additional collateral is needed. However, in the vast majority of the cases, there is a rollout of the loan by the policyowner taking policy loans to repay the bank debt. Usually an irrevocable trust is used to keep the policy proceeds outside the estate.

When people make major purchases like a house or a business, they typically finance most of the transaction. That's because either they don't have enough cash for the entire transaction, or they don't want to part with their investments in the stock market or someplace else. So they finance the purchase.

Similarly, when someone needs a large amount of life insurance, even if they don't have the cash flow to pay the premium, they can finance the premium, or most of it, by having a bank lend them the money to buy the life insurance. Banks absolutely love life insurance as collateral because its value does not vary with the market. When interest rates are low, the cost of getting this financing is also quite low.

> **The single biggest exemption in the tax code is the exemption for life insurance.**

From a planning perspective, if your business can earn on its own more than the cost of financing you will pay to the bank, or if you can earn on the policy more than what you are paying the bank, then you can create arbitrage, or leverage, by using other people's money—in this case, the bank's money—to buy life insurance.

Most people don't think of this solution. They think they have to pay *all* the money themselves. But in many business situations, and often in estate-planning situations where an estate is large but not liquid, such a premium-financing technique can be very useful.

Premium financing is an attractive way to buy life insurance, especially when interest rates are low from the bank.

Many times, financial advisors who are laser-focused on investments ignore one of the most critical elements of a financial plan: insurance. Insurance protects your future income and everything and everyone you treasure. As you seek out a competent financial advisor whom you feel comfortable sharing your financial situation with, please be sure to select one who understands, and is passionate about, the miraculous ways in which life insurance can protect you and your family. An advisor who has completed the Chartered Life Underwriter (CLU) would likely be well suited to guide you on Life insurance matters.

All types of life insurance protect your family and business against loss of income due to death, but a permanent life insurance contract can do much more than that. I like to call permanent life insurance the "Swiss army knife of financial planning." It can provide funding for business and education endeavors, and it can provide long-term-care solutions.

Life insurance can offer protection against the claims of creditors when the insured person dies. And essentially, your insurance policy can be assigned as collateral, if you need to use it for that purpose. The IRS is not in the business of buying homes, businesses, or land and selling them. They want cash. The reason life insurance is a preferred strategy is because it provides the money when a person dies on a tax-free basis. It's a highly efficient solution for estate-planning situations.

There is reason it's called "life insurance" instead of "death insurance." It has significant lifetime benefits. With life insurance, people tend to think that you can only "win" if you die. But that is not true. It's all about designing your financial plan with life insurance in such a way that meets your needs and solves potential problems.

Your financial plan is the important guide that will help you navigate your way through all the uncertainties of life toward retirement. The more complete it is, the better it will serve you as a strategy to address every possible situation you might encounter.

Life Insurance Fills Many Gaps of Protection

As a financial advisor, I see many family situations that exhibit weakness in the planning process. That weak link, or gap, is often a lack of adequate insurance.

A family depends on the primary income earner to bring in regular income that will meet their needs. If he or she does not have life insurance in place, that already terrible situation will put undue financial stress on the surviving spouse and children. How will that family pay the mortgage, school expenses, and other lifestyle expenses?

The solution to this very real threat is to get life insurance in place for the protection of your beneficiaries. It is our experience that most people have some life insurance, whether it's from their employer or an association. But almost 95 percent of the time, we are finding that people don't have *adequate* insurance.

In general, you should have, at a minimum, total life insurance that equals about ten times your annual salary. So, for example, if you earn $100,000 per year, a good guideline is to have at least $1 Million of life insurance on yourself. Typically the lower the interest rates; all else being equal the greater the amount of life insurance needed.

I am not a huge fan of offering rules of thumb because every individual's situation is unique. The reason I offer this general guideline is that one of the most common situations we see is that, sometimes, people are unwilling to share the details of their financial circumstances, especially in terms of debts and mortgages, with an advisor—at least initially. In those cases, we give them a general guideline so they will at least know the minimum amount of protection they need to get in place. Of course, the ideal situation is for us to establish mutually respectful relationships built on trust so that we can learn all the important details about each individual's financial situation. That is the only way we can truly craft a financial plan that solves every problem that individual might face, now or in the future.

Another situation we see often is that people work for companies for decades, but when they retire, they cannot continue the employer-provided life insurance. Obviously, if you don't die before age 65, you're going to die after age 65. In most cases, we find that everyone needs life insurance. None of us knows when we will pass away.

A third situation we see is, on the personal side, many people are supportive of certain causes. They could be charitable or educational causes, such as the American Heart Association, Rotary International, or universities they attended. They attempt to support those causes during their lifetime by making charitable contributions and donations. Over time, those organizations become dependent on that support. When a regular contributor passes away, that valuable support evaporates because that individual's survivors may not have the same degree of commitment to supporting that cause.

My question has always been, if it is important for you to support a particular cause during your lifetime, wouldn't you want to continue to support it when you are dead and gone? I assume you equally entrust to them the perpetuity of that course.

These are all examples of personal situations in which a product called *life insurance* can be used strategically.

Types of Life Insurance

Life insurance comes in many different forms. Let's look at the most common types, and the strategies they offer.

Term Life Insurance

The most common type is *term life insurance.* Often, you will see ads on TV for even the internet or this product. Essentially, it is life insurance for a specified duration, such as 30 years. In effect, if you die during that designated 30-year period, then the insurance company will pay a benefit to your beneficiaries. But if you outlive that term, then you no longer have life insurance. You will have to buy a new policy, subject to your health and medical underwriting at that time. And you will not receive a refund of the money because you outlived the term.

It's kind of like renting an apartment versus buying a home. Most people know intuitively that in the long run, buying a home is better for most people—certainly those in the higher tax brackets—because you build equity, and the after tax-cost is often lower than renting an apartment.

That said if all one could afford is Term Life insurance; it is advisable to obtain the one with longer "convertible" provisions as that can help you convert in the future to Permanent coverage without providing new "evidence of insurability" in case there is a change in health that would otherwise preclude your being able to obtain coverage.

Permanent Insurance

Another common type of insurance is called *permanent insurance.* This type of insurance will last typically until the age of 120. When I first came into the business, the age that companies specified was 95 or 100. But with generally improving mortality and life expectancy, now it goes to age 120.

Permanent policies can be funded in a variety of different ways.

There are flexible premiums that can increase or decrease the death benefit within certain conditions that time permits. For example, you could have a situation in which the cash value, or the accumulation value, of your policy can be aligned with current money rates or to an index like the S&P 500 [2,3] or a variable policy.[4] That is essentially like having a subaccounts, such as one composed of mutual funds, inside the life insurance contract. Just like many of our clients diversify their investment portfolios, some also diversify their insurance portfolios.

Generally speaking, if you want more guarantees, the premiums will be higher. If you want more opportunities, you have to be willing to take some risk. If you are willing to take some risk, everything else being equal, the insurance company will probably be willing to give you a break on the premium and a whole host of possibilities between the two extremes.

One reason that people like to use these permanent policies on an accumulation basis is because of the tax advantages involved with them.

Life insurance is essentially a "zero coupon bond" that matures at age 120 or at death, if it comes earlier than age 120. We all know our date of birth, but none of us knows our date of death, so we should plan for this eventuality. A lot of younger people don't pay attention to this, thinking they don't need to worry about dying because that's a long way away. Or maybe their family has above-average longevity.

The fact is, the earlier you buy your policy, the less expensive it will be, and the more it will accumulate value over time because of the "magic" of compound interest. Essentially, if you understand compound interest, you *earn* it; if you don't understand it, you *pay* it. In other words, as Roger Zener used to say, "There is an age-discrimination plan at work as you get older when it comes to obtaining life insurance." As Irwin Burt Meisel adds, "Beware of bargains in parachutes, toilet paper, life preservers, fire extinguishers, brain operations, bungee cords, and life insurance!"

I actually have eight life insurance contracts on myself. They are all designed for different purposes, and they are funded differently as well. The very first contract I ever bought has been my best-performing policy. It's not the largest one I have, but it is the best one. I am not advising you to put all your money in life insurance, but I do recommend that, to the extent that you have a need for it, you are better off starting it sooner rather than later.

Below is a guideline that might assist in determining suitable contracts depending on the risk level of the consumer:

- **Conservative:** Whole life or no-lapse guaranteed policies
- **Balanced:** Traditional universal life with some guarantees and some risk
- **Aggressive:** Few guarantees or none, such as variable universal life
- **Passive aggressive:** For the investor who wants no downside investment risk but wants a disproportionate amount of upside potential—use indexed universal life.[5]
- **Variations of above:** Depending on client needs, budget, and time horizon; sometimes, blending in some "term and/or paid-up additions riders" meets objectives.

Single People Can Benefit from Life Insurance

Single people tend to think they do not need life insurance, especially if they have not bought a home yet, gotten married, or had kids. But they need to look further into the future. As they work with their financial advisors to build a financial plan that provides financial confidence, they are planning not just for one or two years, but rather for the duration of their lives, which hopefully will be a long time.

We like to make observations 10 years forward. Let's say I am working with a 25-year-old named Julian who is single. If I am making a 10-year-forward observation, I might ask him, "Would it be fair to say that ten years from now, you might be married? Ten years from now, do you think you might have a home with a mortgage? Would it be fair to say that ten years from now, you might have a spouse and children? Is it possible that you might start a business in the next decade?"

If Julian says yes, any or all those situations are possible, then what he is really saying is that even if he doesn't need life insurance today, he *will* have a need for life insurance in the future. I will remind him, "Every year that you wait to buy life insurance, especially in your twenties and thirties, your premium is going to go up."

Premiums can increase 3 to 3.5 percent per year. So if Julian wants to wait 10 years to buy life insurance, then my argument is, "Why not buy it when it's 'on sale' by 35 percent?" Most of us like to buy whatever we can on sale. So why not lock in a lower premium for life insurance now by buying it in advance?

The other big issue is that we never know what our health might be like in 10 years. Even if you are healthy now, in your twenties and thirties, you have no guarantee that you will continue to be blessed with good health forever. The moment you receive a diagnosis of diabetes or heart disease, for example, you could be deemed uninsurable. The earlier you get life insurance, the better!

Personal Applications of Life Insurance

Like anything else, insurance agents and financial advisors get volume pricing with larger placed amounts. You want to work with a company that is well established, that has been around for a long time, because you want to make sure that if you live long enough, the company will be around to pay the benefits. I haven't seen too many failures in the life insurance space; nevertheless, I take comfort in the fact that if we're making a good selection today, it will stand the test of time. I do the due diligence on the financial strength of the various companies whose products I believe in for my clients.

As you will hear me say often, I believe it is critical to design solutions with your own personal situation in mind. Now I want to describe some situations in which I have customized life insurance for people's unique circumstances.

Long-Term-Care Rider[6]

One common situation that families often face is when a disabled or elderly family member needs long-term nursing care. This type of care is extremely expensive in the United States, although the costs vary from city to city. But broadly speaking, most people who need long-term nursing care will experience a significant impact on their finances.

A *long-term-care rider* on your insurance policy is an excellent solution for this situation. The relatively nominal premium is typically a lot lower than a standalone long-term-care policy. For a nominal premium, a long-term-care rider can be added to your life insurance policy. If you need long-term care, many insurance companies will provide a certain percentage, typically 2 to 4 percent per month of the death benefit of your policy.

For example, let's say you have a $1 million life insurance policy that includes a 2 percent monthly benefit for long-term care. The insurance company would allow you to access $20,000 per month for long-term-care expenses, even though you haven't passed away. That $20,000 per month would come off the base amount—in this example, $1 million. If you used that benefit for 10 months at the rate of $20,000 per month, that's a total of $200,000. If you were to pass away at that point, then your beneficiaries would receive the face amount of the policy ($1 million) minus the $200,000 you used for long-term care ($800,000).

The beauty of this type of protection, which is one type of a "living benefits" solution, is that you are passing along the risk of needing long-term care to an insurance company, without buying a separate long-term care policy. And the money is not "wasted" because, essentially, you are either going to die, in which case your beneficiaries get the full benefit, or you will use your life insurance death benefit, in advance, to pay for long-term care. This is a strategy that can help you win, no matter what happens!

Disability Waiver Premium Option

Another situation in which "living benefits" life insurance can benefit you is in the event that you become disabled as the result of an accident or a sickness. In that situation, you should not have to lose your life insurance just because you lost your income.

Most insurance companies offer what is called a *disability waiver premium option* that waives your premium but keeps your insurance policy in force as long as you, the insured, are disabled. Then, when you recover and are no longer disabled, you do not have to pay the back premiums that the insurance company waived or paid while you were disabled.

Guaranteed Insurability Option

Another popular solution, especially for younger people, is called a *guaranteed insurability option*. With this option, you can increase your coverage in the future, regardless of what your health might be at that point. You can use this option to buy more coverage without having to undergo medical exams or underwriting. You will simply pay the premium for more coverage.

Overloan Protection Rider

Another option that some companies offer is called an *overloan protection rider*. This option protects you from a situation in which you take money out of your policy for living benefits or to put a down payment on a home or start a business, and your collateral fluctuates in value. You do not want to have a situation in which your policy lapses and creates a taxable "phantom income." An overloan protection rider protects against that risk.

Return of Premium Rider

Allows for a recovery of all cumulative premiums paid on a tax-free basis. This is often available in permanent insurance as an add-on death benefit and sometimes in term life, at the end of a specified period of time.

How Life Insurance Helps People Be Their Own Banker

Bankers are some of the most astute financial wizards; many bank executives own substantial permanent life insurance, as well as annuities. They know the powerful benefits offered by insurance contracts.

When life insurance is owned by a bank, it is called bank-owned life insurance, or BOLI. When owned by other corporations, it is known as corporate-owned life insurance, or COLI. Because most of these companies are publicly traded, the details of such contracts are disclosed in their financial statements.

But even if you aren't a banker or the owner of a corporation, you can still leverage life insurance to be your own banker.

There are some interesting examples of how well-known people have used this solution. One well-known example is Walt Disney.

Many years ago, when Disney came up with the concept of Mickey Mouse and Donald Duck, he kept drawings of his cartoons in a scrapbook, a notebook. He told his dad that he wanted to make a business out of his drawings. He experienced many creative successes with many different films. Then he had an idea of a theme park. He went to local banks to see if he could get some funding for his idea, but at each bank he visited, the bankers laughed at him and did not give him the funding. When he told his dad about it, his dad said, "Why don't you take a loan against the life insurance policy I started for you?"

So, in 1953, Walt Disney borrowed from his life insurance policy to help fund Disneyland, his first theme park.[7]

The rest is history.

Retailer JC Penney also became his own banker, in essence, by using his life insurance policy for funding. Following the 1929 stock market crash, Penney borrowed from his life insurance policies to help meet the company payroll. If he hadn't had ready access to capital, the company probably would have been forced to close its doors, adding even *more* people to the unemployment line.[8]

I hope you can see how life insurance can be used creatively to solve many different types of problems. It is incredibly versatile. I have helped clients use life insurance as their own bank. Instead of taking out loans to finance their business needs, pay off credit cards, or pay for a college education, they used the cash value of their life insurance policies. You certainly get more favorable terms on your life insurance policy than you will get at a bank. In addition, you have complete flexibility regarding your repayment terms. Plus, when you borrow money from yourself, it doesn't affect your credit score. Therefore, it won't impact your ability to get other credit, such as a credit card.

When you start a bank, you have to capitalize the bank before you can lend money. Banks typically lend $10 for every $1 they have in assets. Banks consider a loan an asset on the balance sheet, and they consider a deposit a liability. If you became your own banker and use life insurance, especially across multiple generations, then over time, you are essentially creating a family bank. Below is a diagram that shows how this might work for you:

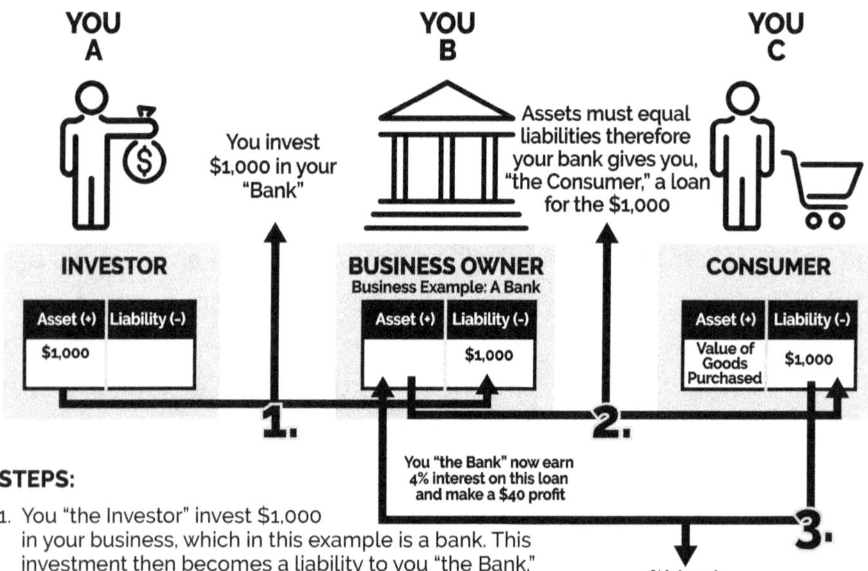

STEPS:

1. You "the Investor" invest $1,000 in your business, which in this example is a bank. This investment then becomes a liability to you "the Bank."

2. Since assets must equal liabilities, you "the Bank," loans you "the Consumer" $1,000 which becomes the consumers liability because the consumer must pay back the loan.

3. You "the Consumer" pay back the loan with 4% interest and this then becomes an asset to "the Bank" by earning a $40 profit.

The above hypothetical example is for illustrative purposes only and is not intended to represent the past or future performance of any specific investment.

Essentially, you wear three hats when establishing a family banking process—one as an investor, the second as business owner, and the third as a consumer. For this typically the ideal contracts are dividend-paying whole life contracts from mutual life insurance companies.

Modified Endowment Contracts[9] Help You Leverage Your Heirs' Assets

Another creative way you can use life insurance to protect your assets is to convert some of your assets into a modified endowment contract (MEC). A MEC can help you protect the assets you leave to your heirs. *This will be helpful only for funds you do not need to use during your lifetime.* However, from a practical point of view we do not advise these contracts as situations often happen to change and for "living benefits" to be optimized without taxation; you want to fund contracts up to but no more than the MEC limit.

A MEC is a tax qualification of a life insurance policy whose cumulative premiums exceed federal tax-law limits. The taxation structure and IRS policy classification changes after a life insurance policy has morphed into a modified endowment contract. In other words, the IRS does not consider it to be a life insurance contract anymore. The change in classification was brought about to combat the use of the "life insurance" designation for the purposes of tax avoidance. Specifically, a life insurance policy is considered a MEC by the IRS if it meets three criteria:[10]

1. The policy was entered into on or after June 20, 1988.
2. It must meet the statutory definition of a life insurance policy.
3. The policy must fail to meet the Technical and Miscellaneous Revenue Act of 1988 (TAMRA) "seven-pay test."

The seven-pay test determines whether the total amount of premiums paid into a life insurance policy, within the first seven years, is more than what was required to have the policy considered paid up in seven years. Policies become MECs when the premiums paid to the policy are more than what was needed to be paid within that seven-year time frame. Life insurance policies entered into before June 20, 1988, are not subject to the payment of premiums over the money allowed under federal laws. However, the renewal of an older life insurance policy after this date is considered new and must be subjected to the seven-pay test.[11]

The illustration below shows how different types of insurance types relate to MECs. At the top of the diagram are MECs—insurance policies that offer 100 percent savings with the least amount of life insurance. At the bottom of the diagram is term life insurance, the cheapest option; it offers only insurance. There is no savings component with term insurance. Almost always, the optimal funding is at the non-MEC limit.

Using these types of accumulation-oriented contracts or investment grade life insurance presents maximum flexibility without negative tax consequences while retaining the "first in first out"' (FIFO) treatment for withdrawals, unlike all other financial products other than the ROTH IRA. No wonder many consider this to be a Jumbo ROTH; it does not have the income tests or the dollar limitations to contribute, as long as it is designed properly. This becomes, effectively, a "family bank."

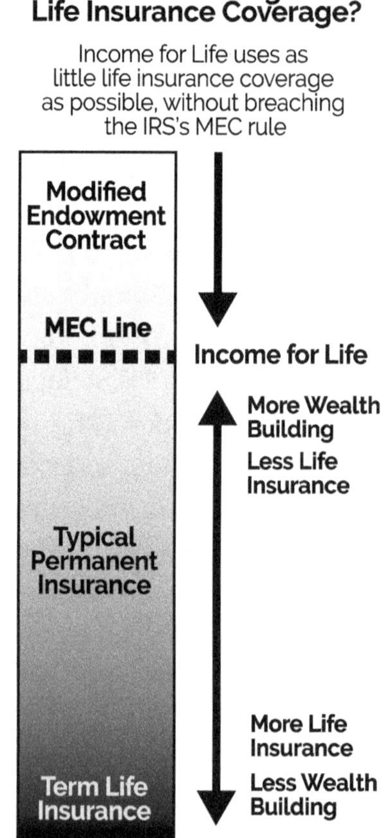

How Life insurance and Investments Complement Each Other

Below is a diagram that shows a hypothetical client with $1 million invested and agrees to contribute 5 percent, or $50,000 into a life insurance contract. Now let's evaluate three different scenarios:

1. His investments do well, and his account value doubles to $2M. In this scenario, the ratio of life insurance premiums declines to 2.5 percent of his portfolio—not a big deal at all from an affordability standpoint.

2. His investments do poorly and decline to $500K, in which case he can use the funds in the life insurance for any needed emergencies or the opportunity to purchase additional investments, since they are an attractive value relative to their intrinsic value.

3. A disaster occurs, and he dies prematurely; in this case, it provides tax-free, immediate funds to the family to replace lost income and maintain their lifestyle.

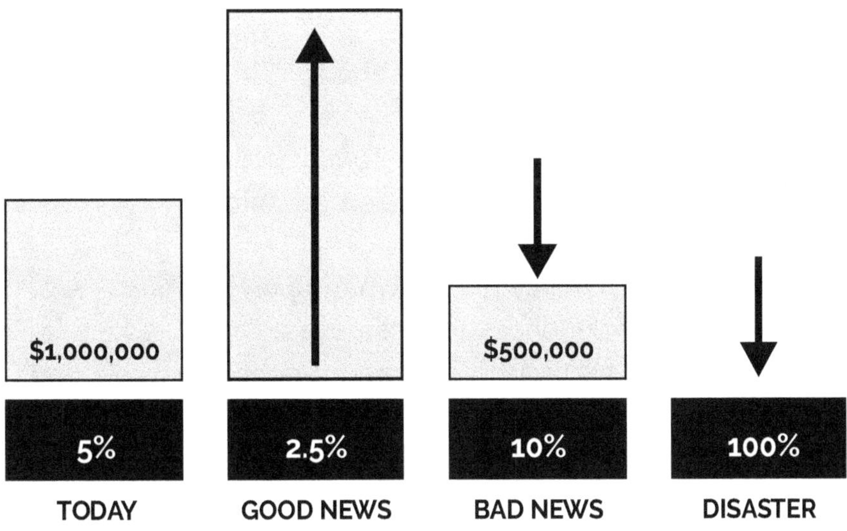

Buy Life Insurance for Your Children

People tend to think of life insurance as a protection product that is necessary to purchase only for an income earner in the family. It is indeed critical to purchase life insurance for adults because a death benefit will fortify the family if that income earner dies unexpectedly. But I also recommend getting life insurance in place for your child. Here are twelve reasons why:

1. **To let your child enjoy the benefit of a low rate.** Everyone knows life insurance premiums increase with age because of the increase in death rates. Every year of delay in taking out insurance means an increase in the cost per dollar of protection, or a reduction in the amount of insurance per premium dollar.

2. **To provide help in learning foresight and thrift.** It is the function of the schools to teach your child to think and to accumulate knowledge. It is the function of the church to teach morals and religion. It is the function of the home to help the child develop a good character and a good personality.

3. **To help in selecting the first policy.** The life insurance way of foresight and thrift represents a long-term transaction. It is important for you to give your child the benefit of your knowledge of the purpose and advantages of the various forms of policies.

4. **To provide a policy that will mature early in life.** One of the happiest experiences that can come to a person is to find that one of his or her life insurance policies has reached the end of the premium-paying period or is maturing for its value as an endowment.

5. **To accumulate enough cash to help with college.** Financing your child's college education may present no problem whatever for you when college time comes. Perhaps ample funds will be on hand. Perhaps not.

6. **To profit by your investment experience.** Do you still have the first investment you ever made? If you have, then you are an exception to the general rule. Most people have to learn their investment lessons in the school of bitter experience and regrettable losses.

7. **To guarantee protection against uninsurability.** If something were to happen to your child—and sometimes things do happen—to make him or her uninsurable, perhaps with a spouse and a child or two as dependents, both of you would rejoice that some insurance had been bought in the early years. Or else you would be remorseful that insurance had not been secured while your child was insurable.

8. **To train your child to bear responsibility.** A policy on your child's life—with the mother as beneficiary—will produce a sense of worth in the feeling that he or she is helping to protect her. And it will give you the assurance that he or she will be prepared to take over the full responsibility, should it become necessary.

9. **To help instill a sense of worth through policy ownership.** You want your child to grow into a person any parent would be proud of. You want him or her to develop character that will win respect.

10. **To help your child be ready to meet financial problems later.** It has often been observed that most financial problems are easily solved if attacked early enough.

11. **To do for your child what you would wish done for you.** The acid test of the wisdom of buying a policy for your child is whether you wish your parents had bought a policy on your life when you were young.

12. **To offset a potential loss.** An insurance policy on the child's life will offset, at least partially, the loss of the investment in his or life and will protect the other members of the family against unnecessary handicaps in the event that death does occur.

If you buy life insurance for your child, he or she will always be covered, regardless of future health. Plus, a permanent life insurance policy for a child can earn cash value. By the time your son or daughter is eighteen and off to college, he or she can use the money to buy a car or help pay for college expenses. Not only that— the premium on the policy you buy for your child now is locked in; it will never change!

This is a strategy to address many potential problems that could arise in the future.

————————

To close this chapter on the power of life insurance, here is an analogy that illustrates its leveraging capacity:

What I'll do:

1. I will work for $10 per hour.
2. After 10 years, you can fire me, and I will give you back everything you have paid me.
3. After 20 years, you can stop paying me, and I will continue to work for you for the rest of your life.
4. When you retire, I will pay you an income.
5. If you need to borrow money, I will either lend it to you or co-sign for up to 90 percent of the wages you paid me.
6. If you become disabled, don't worry; I will pay myself.
7. When you die, I will make a tax-free lump-sum payment to your family and/or business.

Who am I? I am your life insurance policy!

————————

Here is another creative way to depict how life insurance can benefit you in ways that nothing else can:

A Letter to You from Your Policy

I am your policy.

You and I have similar purposes in this world.

It is your job to provide food, clothing, shelter, schooling, medicine, and other things for your loved ones. You do this while I lie in your safe deposit box.

I have faith and trust in you. Out of your earnings will come the cost of my upkeep. At times, I may appear insignificant to you—but someday (and who knows when), you and I will change places.

When you are laid to rest, I will come alive and do your job. I may provide food, clothing, shelter, schooling, medicine, and other things your family will continue to need—just as you are doing now. When your work and labor are done, mine will begin. Through me, your hands can carry on.

Whenever you feel the price you're paying for my upkeep is burdensome, remember that I can do more for you and your family than you will ever do for me.

If you do your part, I will do mine..

Sincerely yours,
Your Policy

Finally, here is a tribute to the Life insurance greats of yesteryears that have contributed to my conviction about it since 1992:

Now I lay me down to snore,
insured for several thousand more.
If I should die before I wake,
my wife would get her first big break.
But should I live for 30 years,
my wife and I need shed no tears.
We can retire, golf, and rest;
back come my bucks in interest.
In old age we can keep our house
and not live with our son's spouse.
So, thank God for the great endurance
of the man who sells life insurance.

Chapter 2 Call to Action:

Secure, at a minimum, total life insurance that equals about ten times your annual salary to protect your family members from the unexpected loss of your income in the event that you die unexpectedly. Also, to preserve your hard-earned wealth and to increase the odds that it will survive into future generations, consider using whole life insurance as the foundation of your own "family bank."

Protecting the Golden Goose

> The only difference between death and
> disability is six feet of ground.

Most individuals, when they start their careers, often do not realize that even if they don't have much in the way of assets and may indeed have significant liabilities—especially if they are saddled with student loan debt—they do have a bright future ahead of them. It needs careful navigation to help ensure financial success.

Fundamentally, there are two ways to make a living:

1. People at work—that is, "You work for your money."
2. Money at work—that is, "You put your money to work for you."

Like any other machine, the human machine is a depreciating asset; we need to invest and save money so someday we can rely on our money working for us by providing adequate income to fund our lifestyle.

However, in the meantime, while we are working and earning an income, we are essentially like a goose that lays a golden egg. This goose needs to be protected to help ensure that, whether due to sickness or accident, the income is reliable for our present needs as well as to provide for future accumulation.

This protection is called *disability income (DI) insurance*, or simply *income insurance.* Often, employers provide some of these benefits on a limited basis. However, it does need to be supplemented. Self-employed individuals or small businessowner will need to obtain this on their own. It is probably the single most important protection a person can have because it protects your most valuable asset: your ability to get up and go to work to generate income.

Disability Income Insurance Protects Your Future Income if You Should Become Unable to Work

DI insurance provides supplementary income in the event that an illness or accident results in a disability that prevents you from working. Typically, benefits are paid monthly, which allows you to maintain the standard of living you are accustomed to and to pay recurring expenses.

In general, DI insurance is designed to replace 45 to 65 percent of your gross income on a tax-free basis. If your policy includes bonuses and commissions, they are provided to you as tax-free income because you used after-tax dollars to pay for your premiums.

Just as life insurance protects future loss of income should you die prematurely, disability income insurance protect future loss of income should you become disabled. The following diagram shows how these products protect your income.

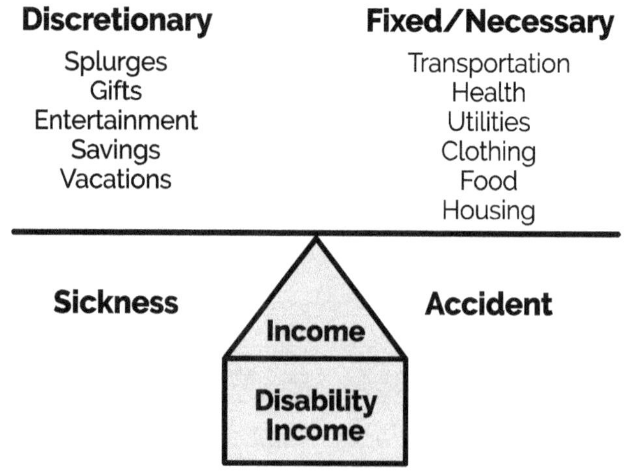

The day you retire, all the rules change. It's now all about *alpha*—retirement alpha, that is. Throughout your career, you have focused on earning and saving money. But planning for retirement goals is dependent on the following four considerations: lifestyle, liquidity, longevity, and legacy.

Compared to your working years, the following concerns are likely to surface during your retirement years:

- Reduced earning capacity
- Visible spending constraints
- Heightened investment risk
- Unknown longevity
- Spending shocks
- Compounding inflation
- Potential decline in cognitive abilities

Essentially, as financial advisors, we manage four stories for our clients who are navigating retirement:

1. Ambiguity
2. Big decisions
3. Complexity
4. End of life

As you respond to these significant issues, the answers to the following two questions will determine your potential for success in retirement:

1. How much guaranteed lifetime income do you have?
2. To what extent have you taken key retirement risks off the table?

Investments can help mitigate many of these concerns. Let's look at how they can help optimize your outcomes. As the legendary Warren Buffett said, "Our favorite holding period is forever."

Investments Can Increase Your Purchasing Power

When you are investing money for what I would consider to be the medium to long term, I believe it is best not to keep that money in the bank or money market accounts. They offer little or no interest and likely won't even keep you ahead of inflation. Instead, we recommend that you invest that money in ways that will grow more than inflation at the very least.

Many people keep their money in cash because they perceive it as a safe option. They figure that if the stock market crashes and they don't have their money in the stock market, then they have dodged a bullet. However, in reality, they are losing purchasing power.

Either you are going to take a risk that you will lose purchasing power, or you are going to take a risk of losing some principal that you contributed. There have been more years of inflation in the history of the United States than deflation. In inflationary times, generally speaking, assets like real estate and company stocks perform better than cash in the bank. Therefore, it is important for you to have the right balance of risk that you are comfortable with. A qualified advisor can help you determine what is a suitable balance of risk for you.

> Over the long haul, there is really no better alternative than equities.

History is a good guide, and history shows that when you invest in equities, you have ownership of a fractional interest in a company or a business. On the other hand, with fixed-income vehicles like bonds, you are effectively loaning money to that business. So you have "loanership." Owners are rewarded for taking that extra risk with a higher return on their money.

We try to build a portfolio in a way that we, hopefully, are not limited to one company, one stock, one industry, or even one country. Better diversification of an equity portfolio over a long period of time can result in a higher return than if you were to invest only in one type of asset.

The higher your return, obviously, the longer your money can last. The following chart shows you how your rate of return affects the longevity of income.

How Many Years Your Money Could Last

RATE OF RETURN

WITHDRAW	1%	2%	3%	4%	5%	6%	7%	8%	9%	10%	11%	12%
12%	7	8	8	8	8	9	10	10	11	11	12	13
11%	8	8	9	9	9	10	10	11	12	13	14	15
10%	9	9	10	10	10	11	12	13	14	15	17	19
9%	10	10	11	11	12	13	14	15	16	18	21	26
8%	11	11	12	13	14	15	16	18	20	24	30	★
7%	12	13	14	15	16	18	20	22	27	36	★	★
6%	14	15	16	18	19	22	25	31	44	★	★	✓
5%	17	18	20	22	24	29	36	★	★	★	✓	✓
4%	20	22	25	28	33	42	★	★	★	✓	✓	✓
3%	25	28	33	39	★	★	★	★	✓	✓	✓	✓
2%	35	40	50	★	★	★	★	✓	✓	✓	✓	✓
1%	★	★	★	★	★	★	✓	✓	✓	✓	✓	✓

SOURCE: Deena Katz, Evensky & Katz/Foldes Financials
NOTE: Assuming the withdrawal will increase to account for inflation after the first 3%
★ Money will never be reduced
✓ Original investment will never be reduced

Of course we cannot predict when or how the market will fluctuate. But here are seven broad strategies that you could take to prepare your portfolio for a turn in the investment cycle:

1. Maintain proper portfolio diversification.[12]
2. Rebalance[13] back to neutral.
3. Shift your mix of equity and fixed income.
4. Move up in quality and duration within fixed income.
5. Rotate toward lower beta equities.
6. Consider implementing alternative strategies.[14]
7. Select investments with better downside characteristics.

How Standard Deviation Is Used to Determine Risk

Many sectors of the finance industry—especially in the investment sector—measure risk to determine the probability that stocks, options, or mutual funds will move in unexpected ways. One way that analysts and traders assess the volatility and relative risk of a potential investments is *standard deviation*. This is a mathematical concept that helps determine the spread of asset prices from their average price.

The following chart shows the average standard deviation by sector:

Average Sector Standard Deviation, 1995–2014:[15]

Consumer Staples	13%
Health Care	15%
Utilities	15%
US Equity Market	16%
Industrials	18%
Consumer Discretionary	19%
Financials	20%
Energy	20%
Telecommunications	21%
Materials	22%
Information Technology	28%

Why Diversification Is Wise: Making the Unknown Known by Using the Familiar

Here are two analogies with visual cues to reinforce the importance of diversifying your portfolio.

1. The Elevator

The diagram depicts two elevators. The first is supported by a single cable, and the second is supported by four cables. Which elevator would you rather be in during an earthquake? We need to apply this same principle to your investments. I want you to have a "four-cable portfolio"—just in case.

2. The Golf Clubs

Holding one investment in a portfolio is like holding only one club in a golf bag. No single investment can help you, the investor, in every market condition. You need a variety of investments, just as you need a variety of different clubs to give you a good chance of navigating the golf course successfully. Most golfers carry 14 clubs in their bags for different conditions. Similarly for financial success you want to have adequate number of asset classes. History shows that 93% of an investment portfolio return is dependent on "asset allocation"[16] rather than the specific security or company chosen.

Three Critical Retirement Events

If you are one of the fortunate few who still have Pension benefits from an employer such as World Bank employees; once you reach retirement, three critical events will occur:

1. Exchange of Checks from a Salary one to a Pension one.
2. The Tough Decision about whether to disinherit the spouse (and get higher pension benefits) or provide spousal benefits (in exchange for a lower pension).
3. The Group Life insurance disaster – when your chances of dying increase this life insurance is either severely reduced or terminated.

The diagram provides a visual representation of this situation:

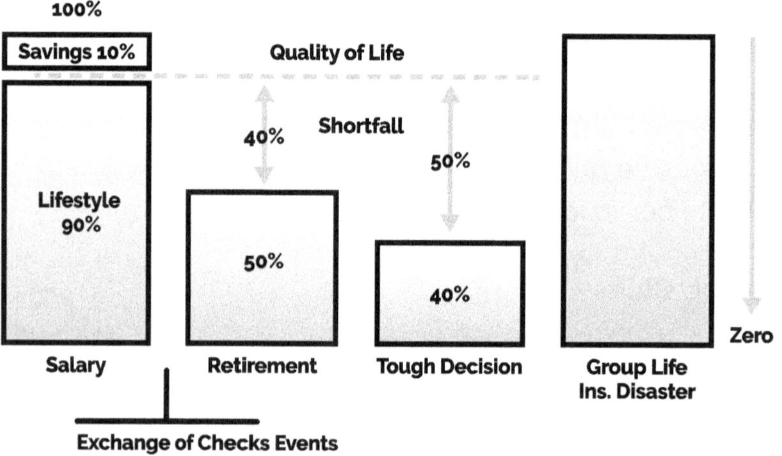

Equities: Higher Risk, Higher Returns

Equities are shares in the ownership of a company. When a company issues *bonds*, it is taking loans from buyers, and when it offers *shares*, it is selling partial ownership in the company.

People invest in equities because of their potential for high returns. In your investing portfolio, your "equity exposure" is another way of describing your exposure to the risk that you will *lose* money when the value of the stocks you own declines. Conventional wisdom states that young people can afford more equity exposure, so they will likely want more stocks in their portfolio because of their potential for returns over time. As you plan to retire, equity exposure becomes more of a risk, which is why many people transition at least part of their investments from stocks to bonds as they get older.[17]

When you invest in equities, you can buy individual stocks, exchange traded funds (ETFs), mutual funds,[18] or some combination of all those. As a general rule, we find that when investors are first starting out and their accounts are smaller in size, they should probably choose mutual funds or ETFs to diversify the risk, given the low amount of investment. As the investment account increases, we can get into more individual securities. The beauty of individual securities in an account is that there are no expense ratios associated with them. Over time, they can actually drive your cost structure down.

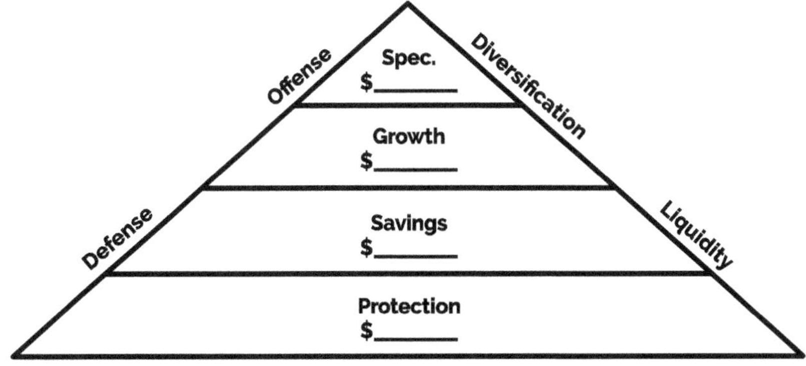

Tax Diversification Is Also Important

Most people hear a lot about the importance of *investment diversification* so their risk is spread out among a lot of different types of assets. For people in high tax brackets, it is equally important, if not more so, to have *tax diversification*.

In other words, I advise them to have some of their money in accounts that are taxed now but will be tax-free later and some money in accounts that are tax-deferred (no tax is due now, but it will be due once they withdraw the funds in retirement).

Tax diversification is an excellent strategy for optimizing your financial outcome.

A critical component of tax diversification is the *location* of your asset.

For example, if you have a bond portfolio that is not in a retirement account, then the earnings from that bond portfolio will be considered taxable income. On the other hand, if you own stocks, particularly growth stock thar are not paying dividends in your retirement account, it will grow and keep growing, and no taxes will be due on that money until you withdraw it. When you do withdraw that money, it will be taxed in full.

Now, what if you switched the situation? If you move your bond portfolio to your retirement account, then interest will accrue on it, but that interest will not be recorded as income every year because it's inside your retirement account. You won't have to pay taxes on that money until you take it out. And when you do take it out, it's unlikely—it's theoretically possible, but unlikely—that your bond portfolio would have grown to the same size as a stock portfolio. So although you have to pay taxes on it at that time, you get two benefits: first, you didn't have to pay tax on that money along the way, and second, the tax on the account will be low.

When you take money out of a stock portfolio, that money will be considered a capital gain, not ordinary income, and you will have to pay a capital gains tax on it. This is because retirement plans are subject to ordinary income tax.

If you purchase investments like stocks and bonds, and then they go up in value and you sell them for a profit, the difference between what you paid and what you sold them for is called "capital gains." The government taxes that money with a capital gains tax. If you invest $1,000 in a mutual fund and you sell that fund twenty years later for $9,000, you will have to pay a capital gains tax on the $8,000 of growth.

Also, the capital gains tax doesn't adjust for inflation. When you sell stocks and bonds twenty years from now, the money you will get will be worth less than it was when you bought them. But the capital gains tax is based on the assumption that the money is worth the same when you sell it as it was when you bought it. That means you will pay more in tax, essentially, than if the tax were adjusted for inflation.

Not only that, but if you die, and the stock in your account has appreciated significantly outside your retirement account, then your beneficiary will get what is called a "step-up in basis." A step-up in basis means there is no taxation of the gains made during that person's lifetime.

Now you can see how *asset location* is a big determinant of how optimized your tax strategies are. It is important to view your investments in that context instead of just focusing on the fact that, for example, you have 60 percent of your investments in equity and 40 percent in bonds, which is what most people do.

> Any politician who says, "I can cut your taxes" is simply bad at math.

A Backdoor Roth IRA Lets High Earners Enjoy Tax Benefits of a Roth IRA

There are a lot of financial products and strategies out there, and each one has a unique set of features. A *backdoor Roth IRA* is an investment strategy that many people are not aware of.

Anyone can contribute to an individual IRA, regardless of income. But not everyone can contribute to a Roth IRA. The IRS determines eligibility on your modified adjusted gross income (MAGI) and tax filing status. In 2019, for example, contributions phased out for single filers with a MAGI of $122,000 or more and for married couples filing jointly with a MAGI of $193,000 or more.

MAGI (Modified Adjusted Gross Income) does not include the following:

- Distributions from ROTH IRAs or ROTH 401(k)s
- Distributions from Health Savings Accounts or Flexible Spending Accounts used to pay medical expenses
- Loans/distributions from cash value life insurance
- Portion of immediate annuity payments in non-qualified accounts
- Proceeds from a reverse mortgage
- Direct charitable contribution of IRA RMDs for those over age 72
- Funds from 529 accounts for educational purposes

But a backdoor IRA is an excellent workaround solution. It enables higher earners to benefit from the tax benefits of a Roth IRA. Let's look at this unique strategy in more detail.

When Is a Backdoor Roth IRA a Good Option?

A backdoor Roth IRA allows anyone, regardless of income, to move money from a traditional IRA to a Roth IRA. Unlike a Roth, there's no income limit for contributing to a traditional IRA.

Most traditional IRAs are deductible, which means you make pre-tax contributions. When you convert these contributions to a Roth IRA the converted amount is fully taxable. Because that could be a big tax liability, most people don't even consider it.

However, you can also have contributions in a traditional IRA that are non-deductible. That means you make them after paying tax and never get to claim a tax deduction for them.

What's interesting is that the IRS allows you to convert non-deductible IRA contributions into a Roth IRA. There's no tax due, except on growth in the account that you earn between the time of contribution and conversion.

If you hold money in a traditional IRA for a short period of time only, the growth and resulting tax should be small. So, this "backdoor" contribution is about the same as making a contribution to a Roth IRA, even if you earn too much to qualify for a Roth.

Potential Problems with a Backdoor Roth IRA

Though sneaking into a backdoor Roth IRA sounds perfect, it doesn't always work as planned. If you already have pre-tax money in a traditional IRA, it presents a problem. For instance, you may have rolled over a 401(k) from an old employer into an IRA or contributed to a traditional IRA on your own.

Here's the catch: when you do a Roth conversion, tax must be prorated over all your IRAs. You can't convert just the non-deductible money and forget about pre-tax amounts.

For example, let's say you have $5,000 in a non-deductible IRA that you want to convert into a Roth IRA. But you also have $15,000 in a pre-tax, deductible IRA.

Because you have a total of $20,000 in IRAs, the $5,000 non-deductible portion is 25 percent ($5,000 / $20,000 = 0.25, or 25 percent), and the taxable portion is 75 percent ($15,000 / $20,000 = 0.75, or 75% percent).

Therefore, you'd have to pay the same ratio of tax on the conversion. So 75 percent of $5,000, or $3,750, would be subject to tax. But if you had only $5,000 of non-deductible money, then you could convert the full amount into a Roth IRA with no tax due.

The point to remember is that if you have a lot of money in a traditional, pre-tax IRA, then a backdoor Roth IRA won't help you avoid tax. The IRS requires you to lump all your IRAs together when you make a distribution and doesn't allow you to cherry-pick one account to convert.

Solution Using a Backdoor Roth IRA

However, there is a possible solution if you really want to do a backdoor Roth IRA and you have a retirement plan at work. You could remove your pre-tax IRA money from the equation by rolling it over into your 401(k) or 403(b). That would leave you with just non-deductible, after-tax IRA money to convert to a Roth.

This strategy only works if your workplace plan allows incoming IRA rollovers, and most do. Plus, you need to be very happy with the investment choices and fees in the plan because you don't have as much control over a 401(k) as you do with an IRA.

If you're self-employed, you could set up a solo 401(k) that allows roll-ins and move your pre-tax IRA money into that plan.

Contribution Limits for a Backdoor Roth IRA

To sum up, you get a backdoor Roth IRA by funding a non-deductible traditional IRA first and then converting it to a Roth. High earners who do this won't qualify to make *new* contributions to a Roth IRA because the annual income limits still apply.

However, once your money is converted to a Roth, it grows tax-free (as opposed to tax-deferred in a traditional IRA), and that could save you a bundle in taxes.

How to Forecast when Your Investments Will Double or Triple

Whatever your investments are, two rules of forecasting are extremely helpful for optimizing your financial outcomes: the Rule of 72 and the Rule of 115.

The Rule of 72: How to Determine when Your Investment Will Double

The Rule of 72 is an easy method for finding how long an investment will take to double based on a fixed annual interest rate. If you divide 72 by your annual rate of return, you can get a rough estimate of how many years it will take for an initial investment to duplicate itself.

Here is an example. Let's say our annual rate of return is 6 percent:

$$72 \div 6 = 12$$

Of course there are no guarantees, but you can project that your money might double in 12 years.

You can also use the Rule of 72 to calculate inflation. Let's say inflation is 3 percent:

$$72 \div 3 = 24$$

That tells us that the cost of anything—even a loaf of bread—will double in 24 years. The number 72 is really the doubling factor. Another way to look at inflation is whatever you can buy for $1 today will cost you $2 in 24 years. In other words, the trading power of your dollar will go down to 50 cents. So that's the rule of 72.

The Rule of 115: How to Determine when Your Investment Will Triple

The Rule of 115 is similar to the Rule of 72, but it helps you project when your money will *triple* instead of double. Divide 115 by the interest rate, and that will tell you how many years it will take for your investment to triple.

For example, if your money earns a 9 percent interest rate, it will triple in 12.78, almost 13, years:

$$115 \div 9 = 12.78$$

Your interest rate can affect your savings significantly. The following example shows the impact of low interest rates. The lower the interest rate you are getting on your money, the longer it will take you to grow that money. Consider how much up-front money it would take to accumulate $100,000 in 20 years, given four different interest rates paid on your money:

- At 1.5% interest: $74247
- At 2% interest: $67,297
- At 3% interest $55,367
- At 4% interest: $45,638

———————

Whether you are calculating your loss of purchasing power, the impact of inflation, or the return on an investment, these rules are very useful in guiding you to plan for the future.

For those who are not interested in too much active investment management but wish to have a long-term investment strategy with a "set it and forget it" approach, our experience suggests that the following might be appropriate for the overwhelming majority of investors:

- Large cap US: 12 %
- Mid-US: 6 %
- Small US: 9 %
- Non-US-developed markets: 11 %
- Emerging markets:[19]   13 %
- Real estate: 7 %
- Commodities:[20]   5 %
- Intermediate US Bonds + TIPS + international bonds: 20 %
- Natural resources: 10 %
- Private equity: 5 %
- Cash: 2 %

For this kind of portfolio, we advise a full rebalance once every four years, which I measure with the presidential election cycle.

Use Dollar-Cost Averaging[21] to Reduce the Cost of Acquiring Assets

Dollar-cost averaging (DCA) is a popular strategy you can use during the accumulation phase of retirement to reduce the cost of acquiring investments.

With DCA, you divide up the total amount to be invested across periodic purchases of a target asset in an effort to reduce the impact of volatility on the overall purchase. The purchases occur regardless of the asset's price and at regular intervals. In effect, this strategy removes much of the detailed work of attempting to time the market to make purchases of equities at the best prices. Dollar-cost averaging is also known as the "constant dollar plan."[22]

Broadly speaking, mutual funds and individual securities can be further segmented by industry, whether it's health care, technology, finance, or a blend. You can buy funds through an advisor. Depending on how the advisor is paid, you might pay a fee for acquiring those funds.

We believe that over a period of time, a financial advisors' fees are more than worth it for most investors. That's because most investors are not in the financial space, and they have a hard time removing emotion from the picture. As a result, they tend to make important financial decisions based on emotion and typically buy and sell at the wrong time. Many investors "buy high and sell low," often as an act of panic, when it should be the opposite: they should "buy low and sell high."

Historically speaking, individual investors do not get returns that are as high as those experienced by institutional money managers. There are exceptions, but we believe that you will be well served by working with an advisor. He or she can help you remove emotion from the picture and maybe prevent you from making a costly mistake.

On most investment accounts, once you get past about $500,000, you will probably pay a fee of 1 percent or lower, and the guidance and support you receive in return is well worth the money.

When you work with your advisor to select your investments, it's important to determine if you are investing for a particular purpose. Regarding money you set aside for health care, many companies offer Health Savings Accounts that offer a tax-deductible way to pay some out-of-pocket health insurance and other health-care costs, including long-term care.

Knowing why you are setting money aside will help your advisor determine the best approach.

As you climb the mountain of retirement, work with your advisor to develop a plan, and follow recommend guidelines. As financial author Tom Hegna notes, a successful retirement strategy should involve the following eight steps for most Americans:

1. Have a *plan*—this is not a DIY project.
2. Maximize Social Security benefits.
3. Consider a *hybrid* retirement.
4. Protect savings from inflation.
5. Secure more lifetime income—the total size of assets is not as relevant.
6. Have a plan for long-term care.
7. Use home equity wisely, including a standby reverse mortgage line of credit.
8. Use life insurance to provide legacy benefits for pennies on the dollar.

Chapter 3 Call to Action:

Consult with a qualified financial advisor to ensure investment diversification, as well as tax diversification.

The Tax Man Cometh

> Taxes are the single biggest factor that will separate people from their retirement savings.

Not all money is taxed the same.

Tax laws are complex. For a proper perspective, the following facts will show you just how lengthy our tax laws are. Consider that there are:

- 272 words in the Gettysburg Address
- 1,458 words in the Declaration of Independence
- 783,000 words in the Bible
- 11,400 words in the tax law of 1913
- 3 million words in the tax law today

It is important to understand the tax implications of every financial move you make, as well as the order of taxation. Your financial advisor will help you avoid marginal tax traps, based on your tax bracket; allocate tax-sensitive assets; consider gifting strategies; deciding what and whom to pay now vs. later; and manage the dynamic bracket results in higher income and lower taxes.

Defined Benefit Plans: The Largest Tax Deduction for Business Owners

The largest single tax deduction available to business owners under the current tax regime is a defined benefit plan. For many small businesses, including self-employed individuals, these plans can offer greater income tax deductions than even defined contribution plans such as 401(k)s, SIMPLE IRAs, and Simplified Employee Pensions (SEPs). They work particularly well for groups of five or fewer employees when the owners are highly compensated, over age forty, and the rank-and-file employees are younger, with much lower compensation.

With 401(k) plans, the contributions are known, but the benefits are unknown because the employee takes the investment risk. In contrast, with a defined benefit plan, the risk is on the employer; the employee is guaranteed a defined pension benefit amount. The employer typically funds the plan by contributing a regular amount, usually a percentage of the employee's pay, into a tax-deferred account.

As a practical matter, many business owners terminate these plans at retirement and then transfer assets to an IRA, which can be invested per their preferences. This can include a guaranteed life income by using a commercial annuity, which is often less expensive than the administrative costs of maintaining the defined benefit plan during the withdrawal phase.

Insured Benefit Retirement Plan

The following chart shows how quickly taxation can erode your money's growth:

If a Dollar Doubled Every Year, What Would Its Value Be in 20 Years?

| | Tax-Free Gains | Gains Subject to 24% Tax | | |
	No Tax on Gains	Amount Each Year	Doubled	Gains After Tax	New Amount to Double
Starting Year $	1	1.00			
1	2	1.00	2.00	0.76	1.76
2	4	1.76	3.52	1.34	3.10
3	8	3.10	6.20	2.35	5.45
4	16	5.45	10.90	4.14	9.60
5	32	9.60	19.19	7.29	16.89
6	64	16.89	33.77	12.83	29.72
7	128	29.72	59.44	22.59	52.31
8	256	52.31	104.62	39.76	92.07
9	512	92.07	184.13	69.97	162.04
10	1,024	162.04	324.07	123.15	285.18
11	2,048	285.18	570.37	216.74	501.93
12	4,096	501.93	1,003.85	381.46	883.39
13	8,192	883.39	1,766.78	671.38	1,554.76
14	16,384	1,554.76	3,109.53	1,181.62	2,736.39
15	32,768	2,736.39	5,472.77	2,079.65	4,816.04
16	65,536	4,816.04	9,632.08	3,660.19	8,476.23
17	131,072	8,476.23	16,952.46	6,441.93	14,918.16
18	262,144	14,918.16	29,836.33	11,337.80	26,255.97
19	524,288	26,255.97	52,511.93	19,954.54	46,210.50
20	$ 1,048,576	$46,210.50	$92,421.00	35,119.98	81,330.48

Note: In 20 years, almost $1 million is lost in taxes.

The above is a hypothetical example that is demonstrating a mathematical principle. It does not illustrate any investment product and does not show past or future performance of any specific investment.

To protect your portfolio from tax erosion, one solution your financial advisor might recommend, based on your situation, is an Insured Benefit Retirement Plan (IBRP). This solution provides seven layers of tax insulation because your income is free from the following:

- Federal income tax
- State income tax
- Local income tax
- Capital gains tax
- FICA/Social Security tax
- Any effect on alternative minimum income tax

- Any negative impact as a consequence of the American Taxpayer Relief Act 2012, patent protection, and the Affordable Care Act
- Any impact on needless taxation of Social Security benefits

Without proper planning, taxes can erode much of the wealth you have worked so hard to accumulate. It is critical that every financial decision you make is made with a focus on minimizing your tax burden. Let's look at more ways to reduce your tax burden.

Forgo Deductions Today to Have a Better Outcome Later

One situation many people are not aware of when it comes to tax planning is that they put money into a retirement plan and take a current-year deduction, not realizing they are potentially creating a huge problem for themselves down the road.

When you are taking a deduction on an investment, realize that the contribution you are making to that investment will be a lot more later, when you withdraw that money, because hopefully, it will grow over time.

For example, let's say you put $25,000 in a retirement plan each year for ten years. Hopefully, by the time you take that money out in retirement, you will have a lot more money than the $250,000 you initially put aside. If it has not grown, it means your investment didn't do well, or your investment advisor didn't do well for you.

When you take that money out later, on the back end, it is going to be fully taxable. Is it better to take a deduction on $25,000 and pay tax in full on $1 million, or is it better to forgo the deduction on $25,000 and not have to pay tax on $1 million? Obviously, nobody knows what the tax rates are going to be in the future. Think about the stimulus the US government paid out in the spring of 2020 following the coronavirus crisis.

Think about the mortgage crisis of 2008, when the government increased the deficit so much. Besides, entitlement programs such as Medicare are like a "fiscal cancer." In fact, according to some studies, Medicare is five times more expensive than Social Security. Somewhere along the line, the tax rates will have to creep up. The current marginal rates are not even close to the highest they have been in our history.

The following graph shows the federal historical marginal tax rates from 1913 through 2020.

History of Tax Rates, 1913–2020[23]

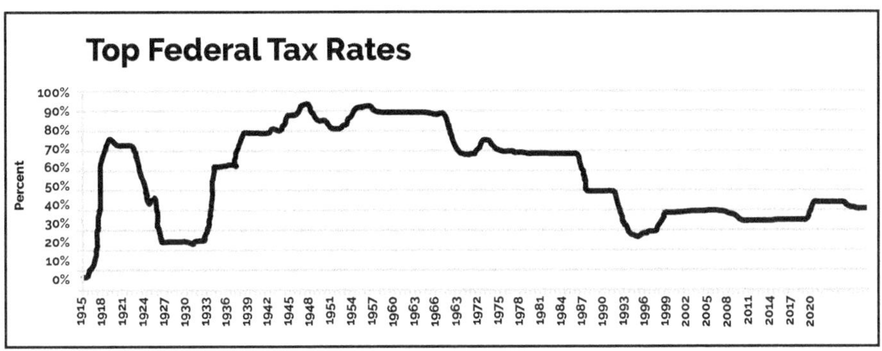

1. As adjusted by the Consumer Price Index Inflation Calculator from the US Department of Labor, Bureau of Labor Statistics, at http://www.bls.gov/data/inflation_calculator.htm.
2. For simplicity, unless otherwise noted, the historical federal income tax rates here refer to the highest tax rate.
3. http://data.bls.gov/cgi-bin/cpicalc.pl
4. http://www.irs.gov/pub/irs-soi/05inrate.pdf, p. 8.

> **The government can get the money it needs by taxing, borrowing, or printing.**

Most of our clients are well-to-do, and in the future, they'll be even better-to-do. Therefore, their tax rate isn't going to go down. In fact, when they retire, they probably will have finished paying off their mortgages, so they won't have the benefit of the mortgage-interest deduction on their taxes.

Business owners who retire and then sell their businesses will no longer have business deductions. Once their kids are grown, they will no longer get exemptions for children. So you can see that often, in retirement, even if your income is the same or a little bit less than it was when you were working, your taxable income could be higher because you've lost all the deductions.

Also, it is important to know that, depending on your total provisional income and your state of residence, up to 85 percent of your Social Security benefits could be taxable.

The point I'm making is that sometimes, it's better to forgo the deduction today so you can have an optimized outcome later.

I have seen people fixate on current-year taxes while failing to plan for taxation in future years. You also have to look at taxation of assets to the next generation, or maybe the next two generations. That requires strategic planning based on your own personal goals. This is a critical conversation, and we believe financial advisors need to address it with their clients. We want to make sure we focus on the future as well as the present and not just what's already happened— last year's income, for example.

Our team focuses on what can we do now so that the outcome for you and your family will be optimized five, ten, or fifteen years down the line, and into the next generation. We collaborate with CPAs, estate-planning attorneys, and any other experts who are integral to helping to optimize your outcome.

We encourage everyone to think about the future—beyond your current situations.

A Depressed Market Can Offer Opportunities

You have to be opportunistic. When the market is in a downturn, it presents a great opportunity for clients whose portfolios have been beaten down to do something called a *Roth conversion*. This is a great solution, and it is an option I present to clients when we are experiencing a depressed market. In some cases, it is wise to convert money into a Roth IRA. Even though you will have to pay tax on that money today, you will be able to benefit when the economy rebounds, and then the appreciation and the distribution in the future will be tax-free.

There will always be changes in tax law, and we will navigate them. I strongly encourage you to seek out the advice of a competent, compassionate, independent financial advisor to help you ensure you are optimizing your tax situation.

Seven Deadly ~~Sins~~ (Taxes) You Can Avoid by Using an Insured Benefit Retirement Plan

A properly crafted supplemental retirement plan funded with a non-MEC (Modified Endowment Contract) permanent life insurance plan optimized for accumulation will provide preferential tax treatment via insulation from the following:

1. Federal income tax
2. State income tax
3. Local income tax
4. Capital gains tax
5. FICA/Social Security tax/Medicare tax
6. There is no effect on the alternative minimum tax (AMT), and
7. Can be free of Estate and Gift taxes.

Minimize Estate Taxes[24] by Using Life Insurance

When wealthy people pass away, their estates are subject to taxation.

An *estate tax* is a levy on estates whose value exceeds an exclusion limit set by law. Only the amount that exceeds that minimum threshold is subject to tax. These levies are assessed by the federal government and about a dozen state governments. They are calculated based on the estate's fair market value, not on the amount the deceased person originally paid for its assets. There may also be a tax levied by the state in which the deceased person was living at the time of his or her death. Under what is known as the *unlimited marital deduction*, the estate tax does not apply to assets that will be transferred to a surviving spouse. However, when the surviving spouse who inherited an estate dies, the beneficiaries may then owe estate taxes if the estate exceeds the exclusion limit.[25]

Let's say an estate is worth $15 million. With the 2020 exclusion limit of $11.5 million, federal estate taxes would be owed on less than $4 million of the estate.

Since my entry into this business in 1983, the estate tax has fluctuated up and down. In fact, there was time when there was no estate tax. Tax laws often change according to who is in the White house and which political party is in the majority.

Again, we can use life insurance in creative ways to minimize the estate tax.

Here is a great example of how that works. Jack Kent Cooke was the owner of the Washington Redskins. The lifelong dream of his younger son, John Kent Cooke, was to own the Redskins. But when the elder Cooke passed away in 1984, his son was not able to assume ownership of the team because his father had not done adequate estate planning.

George Albright, a trusts and estates lawyer in Washington, DC, and a former chairman of the Virginia State Bar's trusts and estates board of governors, said about Jack Kent Cooke's will, "It's the most bizarre will I've ever seen." Cooke puzzled lawyers by choosing to leave the bulk of his money and his prized football team to the foundation instead of to his son, John Kent Cooke; cutting his widow, Marlene, out of the will only weeks before he died; and deleting the names of others who were included in earlier versions of the will.[26]

And when a person dies and money is owed to the IRS, the IRS wants your best asset, not your worst asset. The Cookes essentially had to sell the Redskins to satisfy the estate tax obligation to the IRS.

Estate taxes are due only when the second spouse of a married couple passes away. That's because when one spouse passes away, the other spouse is usually the beneficiary of the entire estate of the decedent.

In practical terms, couples often go on vacation together. They drive together, and they fly together. If an accident happens, it's entirely possible that both spouses could die at the same time. When the second spouse of a couple dies, the estate tax is generally payable within nine months of that person's death.

Selling Real Estate to Pay Estate Taxes

Sometimes people are forced to sell real estate to pay estate taxes. In the example shown below, estate tax in the amount of $10 million is due. When the investor sells real estate to pay the tax (Plan A), he or she is able to come up with the entire amount due— $10 million. But with Plan B, the investor uses life insurance, with an annual capital transfer for ten years, and comes up with only $2 million of the $10 million estate tax that is due.

Selling Real Estate to Pay Estate Taxes

$10,000,000 Estate Tax

Plan A - Sell Real Estate		Plan B - Use Life Insurance	
Market Value	$40,000,000	Annual Capital Transfer	$200,000
Payoff Mortage	-28,000,000	For 10 Years	X 10
Net	$12,000,000	Total Funding to Pay Taxes	$2,000,000
Commissions (5% x 40,000,000)	-2,000,000*		
Net Available to Pay Taxes	$10,000,000		

Note: Selling real estate results in the loss of property, growth and income and incurs commissions. The total insurance funding in this case is equal to the commissions alone paid on the real estate sale.

Irrevocable Trusts Can Help You Manage Estate Taxes

Another way to minimize the amount of taxes your estate incurs upon your death, or upon your spouse's death, is to create an *irrevocable trust*—a trust that cannot be changed or canceled after the document has been signed. This sets it apart from a *revocable* trust, which can be altered or terminated and becomes irrevocable only when the trust maker, or grantor, dies.

You also can use an irrevocable trust to protect assets from being wasted or misused or to protect the assets of an individual who has a disability.[27]

When you set up an irrevocable trust, you give up control of the assets placed in the trust. This creates a completely separate tax entity because the trust isn't managed or controlled by you, the grantor, and it's not yet controlled by your heirs or beneficiaries. The trust pays its own taxes, and it is typically managed by a trustee.[28]

If you set up an irrevocable trust, put funds into it that you will not need to use during your lifetime because you will not be able to get those funds back.

You can put money into the trust that the trustee can use to pay the premiums on a life insurance policy. This will keep that insurance policy outside your own personal assets and provide tax-free liquidity for estate tax purposes. That means your beneficiaries will not have to sell homes, businesses, or other assets.

Chapter 4 Call to Action:

Now that you are familiar with not only income tax but also estate tax matters and some possible solutions to mitigate or eliminate negative consequences; have a discussion with your financial, legal and tax advisors as part of a collaborative team to determine the customized solution appropriate for your situation and get them installed sooner than later to get ahead of any possible detrimental changes in tax laws.

Climbing the Retirement Mountain

> Pre-retirees and the retired need to ask themselves these questions: "What do I want my money to do while I am alive? What do I want my money to do when I die?"

Your *retirement plan* is the bridge that will allow you to transition from your working years into your retirement years. One you have built that bridge, you must protect it from various risks, such as taxation. This is too important to be a "do-it-yourself" project. I strongly recommend that you work with a competent, trusted financial advisor as you plan your retirement.

There are two stages of retirement planning: the *accumulation* phase, when you are putting money away, and the *distribution* phase, when you are taking money out of your retirement accounts once you've retired. These phases require different strategies.

An analogy I like to use is climbing a mountain. Attempting to reach the top of a mountain can be a difficult uphill climb. But most mountain-climbing accidents actually happen on the way down, not on the way up. Many times, this happens because the climber is careless or exhausted.

It also can happen because the climber tries to use the same strategy to descend the mountain that he or she did to climb the mountain. But two very different strategies are required to do both successfully.

This is true with retirement, too. The strategies you use during the accumulation phase of retirement are different from those you need to use during the distribution phase. This is particularly important for people in the "retirement red zone" to recognize. Those are people within five to seven years of the retirement. Age is only a number, but generally speaking, these are people between the ages of 50 and 70.

Your retirement strategy should be unique to your own financial situation. But unfortunately, some financial advisors give their clients general rules of thumb. For example, many will recommend that clients take out 4 percent of their investment portfolios for the rest of their lives, once they retire.

This strategy doesn't take into consideration each client's unique needs, dreams, and reality. And many Americans don't have enough assets accumulated to do that. That approach does not apply to those who rely on Social Security for most or all of their retirement income.

Planning for the future is critical. If you do not develop a plan to optimize your financial outcome for retirement, you run the risk of living a lifestyle that is less enjoyable than you would like.

> **"Most people do nothing wrong; they do nothing, and that's what is wrong."**
> **—Ben Feldman**

Stress-Test Your Retirement Plan

A retirement income plan must address the risks and uncertainties of retirement. These risks include the following:

- Longevity risk
- Early death of a partner
- Rising health-care costs
- Increased need for health care
- Expense of long-term care
- Impact of market volatility
- Sequencing of returns risk
- Liquidity risk
- Inflation risk
- Tax risk

The Accumulation Phase of Retirement

The accumulation phase of retirement focuses on encouraging you to save to meet a targeted amount. The investment recommendations center on maximizing return within your risk-tolerance parameters. The decumulation process is entirely different. The focus is on ensuring that you can meet your income needs and maintain the standard of living you have grown accustomed to throughout your lifetime.

Even the risk/return paradigm is different in retirement income planning. *Return* is measured as the amount that can be withdrawn from the portfolio each year, and *risk* is the possibility that the portfolio will be exhausted before the end of your life.

I am aware that most planners are familiar with the tactics and strategies for the accumulation phase of retirement. They are far less familiar with the vastly different process of planning for retirement-income optimization. Carrying forward the same accumulation strategies into decumulation planning will not be successful.

The trusted advisor you choose to work with needs to be familiar with a wide range of strategies used to create and protect retirement income, including the following:

- A systematic withdrawal strategy—Choosing appropriate withdrawal rate
- Lifetime income annuities—Understanding the implications of mortality credits
- Longevity insurance—Increasing portfolio sustainability
- Deferred annuities with "living benefit" riders—Knowing how they allow for growth and protection
- Multiple portfolios—Creating buckets of portfolios for different time periods or concerns
- Non-insurance approaches—Knowing about mutual fund income plans, TIPS, structured products, etc.
- Long-term care—Understanding funding methods, including insurance
- Medicare supplement options—Knowing how they can control retiree health costs
- Life insurance—Knowing how to use life insurance to provide for survivor income and/or legacy objectives
- Techniques to protect assets from claims of creditors—For example, incorporation
- Strategies for maximizing Social Security benefits—Choosing the right start date
- Reverse mortgages—Being able to recommend when to tap into home equity to meet income or liquidity needs

Is a Reverse Mortgage Right for You?

A *reverse mortgage* is a loan that can be taken out by homeowners who are age 62 or older and who have considerable home equity. In essence, you are borrowing against the value of your home, and you will receive funds as a lump sum, fixed monthly payment, or line of credit. However, with a reverse mortgage, you are not required to make any loan payments. Instead, your entire loan balance becomes due and payable when you die, move away, or sell your home.

In certain circumstances, the proper and creative use of a reverse mortgage can enhance retirement outcomes. Here are some examples of ways to do this:

1. Refinance your regular mortgage to eliminate monthly mortgage payments (although you will still have to pay taxes, insurance, and maintenance). This allows for a guaranteed increase in the unused portion of your credit line.
2. Get standby portfolio protection—Use a reverse mortgage to enhance cash flow in economic down times. This could make all your investments last longer, while your net worth will not necessarily decrease.
3. Replace the need for a cash-reserve bucket. Home loans are not usually taxable. Plus, your cash flow can increase.
4. Purchase needed insurance or investment solutions because of the change in cash flow. Life insurance can multiply your family's wealth.
5. Purchase long-term-care insurance, or use the equity for similar expenses in case you become uninsurable.

During the accumulation phase of retirement, when you are building up your savings, it is important to optimize your ability to get the highest return on your money. It is also critical to work with your financial advisor to minimize your tax burden. Every financial move you make can have tax consequences. Even one mistake can be extremely costly.

For example, money in a regular brokerage account will be subject to capital gains tax treatment, but money in some types of retirement accounts will be tax-deferred until you take that money out during retirement. We also believe in tax diversification of your investments.

It is also important to manage your investments well by rebalancing your asset mix at appropriate and ideal times. If you are investing on a regular basis, rebalancing can help you optimize the assets in your portfolio.

For people who are age 65 or older, we need to focus on solutions that will address income needs, asset allocations, and solutions. The diagram below summarizes this process.

Retirement Income Planning Fulcrum (Age 65+)

	Income Needs	Asset Allocations	Solutions		
		Equity/Fixed Income			
		RED ZONE			FEAR
Decumulation	Insufficient Resources	70/30	Must annuitize all assets	Must export all income risk	
		Greater than 6% Anuuity Rate			
		GRAY ZONE			
Decmulation or Accumulation	Sufficient Resources	60/40	Partial Annuitization	Must export income risk	
		4% or less sustainable withdrawals			
		GREEN ZONE			HOPE
Accumulation	Ample Resources	50/50	Can remain liquid	Can retain income risk	

- Evaluate strategy every Presidential election year
- Assumes provision of legacy objectives via life insurance
- Assume long term care risk has been transferred
- Use QLAC to reduce RMD and expand tail income

The Distribution Stage of Retirement

The distribution phase of retirement is critically important because it is in this phase that you must manage the taxation of your investments. If you make mistakes after you're already retired, you have most likely already stopped working and cannot build up your accounts again.

If you own a traditional IRA, SEP, or SIMPLE individual retirement account, you must make a required minimum distribution (RMD) once you reach a certain age.

On December 20, 2019, the Setting Every Community Up for Retirement Enhancement Act of 2019 (SECURE Act) became law. This act made major changes to the RMD rules. If you reached the age of 70½ in 2019, the prior rule applied, and you had to take your first RMD by April 1, 2020. If you reached age 70½ in 2020 or later, you were required to take your first RMD by April 1 of the year after you reach 72.[29]

During the first part of 2020, retirees were required to withdraw money from their retirement accounts by April 1 following the year that they reached age 72. Once the COVID-19 pandemic hit, President Trump signed the $2 trillion Coronavirus Aid, Relief, and Economic Security (CARES) Act into law on March 27, 2020. This act suspended the RMDs from retirement accounts in 2020 to allow such accounts more time to recover from stock-market downturns.

For defined contribution plan participants, or Individual Retirement Account (IRA) owners, who die after December 31, 2019, (with a delayed effective date for certain collectively bargained plans), the SECURE Act requires the entire balance of the participant's account be distributed within ten years. There is an exception for a surviving spouse, a child who has not reached the age of majority, a disabled or chronically ill person or a person not more than ten years younger than the employee or IRA account owner. The new 10-year rule applies regardless of whether the participant dies before, on, or after, the required beginning date, now age 72.

Your required minimum distribution is the minimum amount you must withdraw from your account each year. You generally have to start taking withdrawals from your IRA, SEP IRA, SIMPLE IRA, or retirement plan account when you reach age 72 (70 ½ if you reach 70½ before January 1, 2020). Roth IRAs do not require withdrawals until after the death of the owner.[30]

You can withdraw more than the minimum required amount.

Your withdrawals will be included in your taxable income except for any part that was taxed before (your basis) or that can be received tax-free (such as qualified distributions from designated Roth accounts).

The Three Phases of Retirement

I see people go through three phases of retirement:

- Phase 1 is the **Go-Go phase**, when people are active. They travel the world. They buy expensive toys like a boat or a plane. They pursue all those experiences, activities, and excursions they never had time for during their careers.
- Phase 2 is what I call the **Slow-Go phase**. This is when people mellow down. They are settled, and their expenses aren't as high as they were before.
- Phase 3 is the **No-Go phase**, when people have significantly curtailed their activities. They might even be incapacitated, maybe in a nursing home, which is incredibly expensive, and they eventually pass away.

Phases 1 and 3 are more expensive than Phase 2. Recognizing this reality, you and your financial advisor might design a strategy whereby you take a higher distribution from your retirement accounts during Phase 1, a little less during Phase 2, and you might need more during Phase 3.

The important question that comes next is, where are you going to get this money from to fund these three phases of retirement? Your answer to that question determines the solution to funding your entire retirement.

People have different ideas about money and different levels of *risk tolerance*—how conservative or aggressive they are with their investments. Although returns are never guaranteed, you can realize a higher return on your investment by investing more aggressively. And you can lessen your risk of losing money in the event of a stock market by investing more conservatively.

Because people have different levels of risk tolerance, their plans are all over the map. Some people think the stock market is going to crash, so they keep all their money in cash. That strategy does not allow them to take advantage of compound interest that builds over time. Others feel that they're going to live a long time, so they continue to invest aggressively in the market at a point when maybe they should start taking less risk.

> **Risk is always equal to historical volatility.**

Managing Risk During Retirement

Once you reach the distribution phase of retirement and are no longer drawing an income, it is more important than ever to manage risk. According to Ed Slott, CPA, the three biggest risks to financial security in retirement are as follows:

1. **Tax risk**—we should manage investments on the way in but manage taxes on the way out.
2. **Investment risk**—especially Sequence of Returns risk
3. **Longevity risk**—This is a multiplier of all risks because the planning horizon is unknown.

We use what we call "the ART formula" for managing risk. ART is an acronym that stands for the right balance among three factors: avoidance (A), retention (R), and transfer (T).

How we do this depends, in part, on whether we want to maximize spending or giving. If your goal is to maximize retirement spending, then we must include annuities as part of your solution. If your goal is to maximize giving, then we must include life insurance as part of your solution.

Our experience suggests that for most clients, it is a combination approach. During the Go-Go Years, people typically have higher expenses; during the Slow-Go Years, expenses tend to be lower; and during the No-Go Years, expenses often increase primarily due to long-term care and other health costs.

Most investors have a high proportion of their investments in fixed-income bond portfolios during the retirement stage of life. But by replacing them with an annuity, they would be effectively getting the benefits of a AAA bond with a CCC yield and a *zero* standard deviation.

A *fixed annuity*[31] is an insurance contract that guarantees that the insurer will pay the purchaser a guaranteed, fixed interest rate on his or her contributions to the annuity for a specific period of time. Fixed annuities generally carry a lower risk than variable annuities and can provide a steady stream of income during retirement. Fixed annuities are the simplest and most straightforward type of annuities.[32]

A qualified and competent financial advisor can help you design, build, and protect your bridge to retirement.

Manage Your Fixed and Variable Expenses

Part of figuring out how much money you will need in retirement is to anticipate what your expenses will be. Most people have both *fixed expenses*—those that will be the same every month—and *variable expenses*—those that vary, are unexpected, or are one-time costs.

For fixed expenses, you should have a guaranteed source of income. For example, if you are still paying on your mortgage and it's $1,000 per month, you need a guaranteed source of income to cover that expense. It will be due every month at a certain time.

Your investments can cover variable, or discretionary, expenses. So, for example, if you want to take all eight of your grandchildren to Disneyland, do so only if you have enough money in your investment accounts.

Overestimate How Long You Will Live After You Retire

I have quantified eighteen different risks people face in retirement. Some of these are well known, such as market risk, interest-rate risk, and inflation risk.

But by far, the most important risk is the *longevity risk*—the risk of outliving your savings—because the longer you live, the longer you are exposed to the other risks.

For decades, Americans' life expectancy increased. Between 1959 and 2016, US life expectancy increased from 69.9 years to 78.9

years. But then US longevity began to decrease. By 2014, midlife mortality was increasing across all racial groups, caused by drug overdoses, alcohol abuse, suicides, and a diverse list of organ system diseases.[33]

That is a troubling trend. None of us knows how long we will live. The last thing you want to do is underestimate the number of years you will live in retirement. It is common for people in their mid-sixties to live in retirement for thirty years.

Manage Your Taxes During Retirement

Taxes will play a big role in the strategy you and your financial advisor will take to fund your retirement. Minimizing your tax burden on your investments is so important that I strongly recommend working with a competent advisor whom you trust. Advisors are savvy about tax laws, which change often. A single mistake in this area can cost you dearly.

An example can help illustrate this concept. Let's say Sarah has estimated that she will need $5,000 per month in retirement, and her investments total $500,000. If Sarah lives for 30 years in retirement, that's 360 months. If she spends $5,000 per month for 360 months, that's a total of $1.8 million. Her estimated monthly expenses are not sustainable.

Many Americans have been getting a paycheck every two weeks for decades. Imagine no longer having that paycheck come in. As a financial advisor, my job is to design a strategy that converts your *paychecks* into playchecks (to borrow a term from Tom Hegna, author of the 2011 book *Paychecks and Playchecks: Retirement Solutions For Life*). In retirement, you should be able to cover your expenses, regardless of how the stock market performs.

Use the Bucket Strategy to Earmark Money for Different Expenses

A common approach to saving is the "bucket strategy." You put aside money for three different types of expenses:

- **Bucket #1:** Money that is invested very conservatively, for near-term use
- **Bucket #2:** Money that is invested somewhat more aggressively, for medium-term use
- **Bucket #3:** Money that is invested quite aggressively, for long-term use

Wait as Long as Possible to Begin Taking Social Security

You can begin taking your Social Security benefits once you turn 62, but we recommend that you wait until your full retirement age, which is typically age 66 or 67, depending on your birth year.

The latest you can begin taking the benefits is age 70. You will increase your Social Security benefit by 32 percent by waiting until age 70 to sign up. For every year you delay taking Social Security benefits, your payment will increase by about 8 percent per year. I will take an 8 percent guarantee over an uncertain return on investment any day.

In 2018, approximately 31 percent of women and 27 percent of men signed up for Social Security as early as possible—at age 62—down from around 54 percent of women and 50 percent of men in 2005, according to Social Security Administration data. Just over one-third of men (36 percent) and almost one-third of women (31 percent) sign up for Social Security benefits at their full retirement age or have their disabled worker benefit automatically converted to a retired worker benefit upon reaching their full retirement age.[34]

If your full retirement age is 66 and you start taking your benefits at age 62, your payments will be 25 percent smaller than if you waited. If your full retirement age is 67 and you start taking the benefits at age 62, your payments will be 30 percent lower than if you waited.

For example, if you are eligible for a $1,200 monthly Social Security benefit at your full retirement age of 66 but start receiving the benefits at age 62, you would get just $900 per month. Imagine trying to live on $900 per month. Not many people could do it easily, especially if they are still paying on a mortgage. As long as you are in decent health, I advise that you wait.

Because Social Security benefits are to be paid in the future, the government is able to make adjustments in the present. Over the next 75 years, the federal government has promised benefits to Social Security recipients in excess of anticipated payroll tax revenues equal to $10 trillion. The Congressional Budget Office estimates that the Social Security shortfall will be equal to 0.75 percent of GDP. With increasing life expectancy, combined with a falling ratio of workers to beneficiaries, Social Security will need to be modified.

What About All Those Trillions of Unfunded Liabilities? The Reality of Social Security

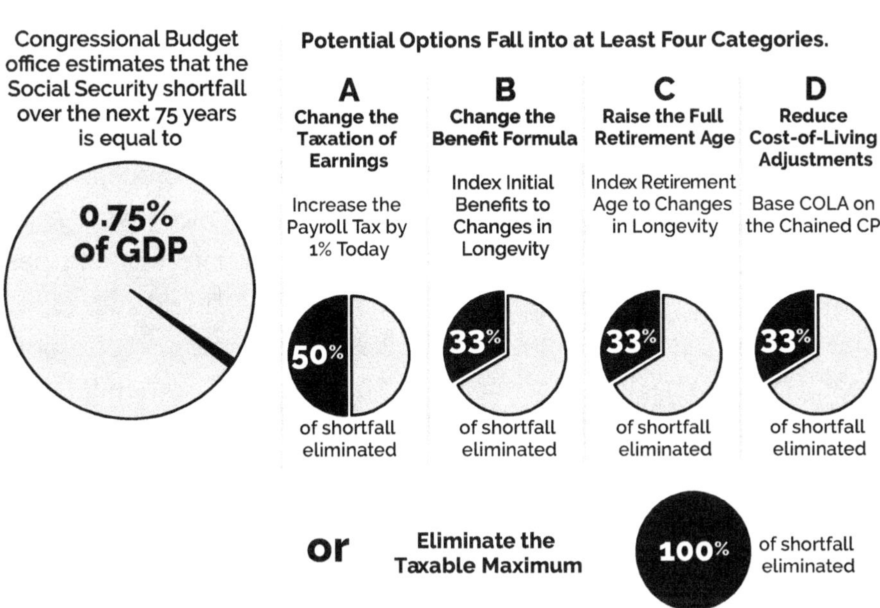

Based on the previous diagram, here are some possible changes the government could make to this program:

- Change the taxation of earnings by increasing the payroll tax.
- Change the benefit formula by indexing initial benefits to changes in longevity.
- Raise and index the full retirement age to changes in longevity.
- Reduce or modify the formula for cost-of-living adjustments.
- Eliminate the taxable maximum.

Stay Active and Engaged Once You Retire

Many of our clients are enjoying what I call a "hybrid retirement"—they are getting some free time while working part-time doing something they enjoy. Some of them are consultants, and some own businesses. People who remain engaged and active once they retire tend to live longer, healthier, and happier lives.

In 2017, the U.S. Bureau of Labor Statistics reported that 32 percent of people ages 65 to 69 were still working, and 19 percent of people ages 70 to 74 were employed. By 2024, it is projected that 36 percent of people ages 65 to 69 will be in the labor force, far more than the 22 percent who were working in 1994. As long as the job is not too physically demanding, stressful, or boring, working past retirement age can result in significant health benefits. Studies show that working past retirement age can lessen the likelihood of serious health problems such as cancer, heart disease, and dementia.

Added benefits of continuing to work a little in retirement is that you won't deplete your savings as quickly, and the health benefits of continuing to work can reduce your risk of needing long-term care.

The SECURE Act Has Changed the Retirement Landscape

For example, on December 20, 2019, President Donald Trump signed the SECURE Act into law as part of the year-end appropriations package.[36]

This is the first major retirement plan legislation since the Pension Protection Act of 2006. Its provisions are meant to increase Americans' access to tax-advantaged accounts and prevent older Americans from outliving their assets.[37]

Here are just some of the ways the SECURE Act will affect your retirement:

1. The Act pushes back the age at which retirement plan participants need to take required minimum distributions (RMDs), from 70½ to 72. It also allows traditional IRA owners to keep making contributions indefinitely.
2. The Act mandates that most non-spouses inheriting IRAs take distributions that end up emptying the account in 10 years.
3. The Act allows 401(k) plans to offer annuities.
4. The SECURE Act will make it easier for small business owners to set up "safe harbor" retirement plans that are less expensive and easier to administer.
5. Many part-time workers will be eligible to participate in an employer retirement plan.

A lot of people are under the mistaken belief that when they get to retirement, they will be in a lower tax bracket. But the reality is that when most people get to retirement, their homes are paid off, and they no longer have deductions for business expenses or for their kids' school expenses. So assuming they have an adequate nest egg, they aren't likely to be lower tax bracket than they were before retirement.

They might even be in a higher tax bracket, and suddenly, they find that they are paying the highest rates for Medicare because Medicare is a means-tested program based on income. Many of these people have a significantly disproportionate amount of their assets in tax-qualified plans like 401(k) accounts. These programs offer an excellent way to put funds aside for retirement over their careers. However, they can contribute to a high provisional income, which is a determinant of the Medicare means testing.

One way to get around all of that is to tap into the cash value of life insurance, which is excluded from the provisional income calculation. Now, with Roth IRAs or Roth conversions, you would have to pay the tax with after-tax dollars. What it comes down to is, would you rather pay tax on the seed or on the harvest? Just as underfunding retirement is a detriment, overfunding can be a detriment as well.

Again, every decision you make as you climb the retirement mountain can have a significant impact on your ability to retire comfortably.

Chapter 5 Call to Action:

Determine where you will get the money to fund the Go-Go, Slow-Go, and No-Go phases of retirement, and begin using the "bucket strategy" to save money for retirement. Overestimate how long you will live after you retire.

Would You Rather Be a Vanderbilt or a Rockefeller?

> It is not about how much money you make; it is about how much of a difference you make.

When you engage in wise and thoughtful planning, you are more likely to optimize your overall financial outcome—during your life and beyond. Those whose legacies endure through generations are typically those who have made prudent decisions about their financial situations during their lifetimes.

Consider the vast difference in the legacies of two well-known American families: the Vanderbilts and the Rockefellers.

Vastly Different Outcomes for the Vanderbilts and Rockefellers

Knowing how to take advantage of the benefits of various financial products, including life insurance, can have a significant impact on your business for generations to come. Let's compare the outcomes of two families, the Vanderbilts and the Rockefellers.

Cornelius Vanderbilt was born into humble circumstances on May 27, 1794, on Staten Island, New York. His parents were farmers, and his father also made money by ferrying produce and merchandise between Staten Island and Manhattan in his two-masted sailing vessel, known as a *periauger*. As a boy, Cornelius worked with his father on the water. When he was a teen, he transported cargo around the New York harbor in his own periauger. Eventually, he acquired a fleet of small boats and learned about ship design.[38]

Cornelius Vanderbilt made his money in the steamships business before investing in railroads. In 1817, he went to work as a ferry captain for a wealthy businessman, Thomas Gibbons, who owned a commercial steamboat service that operated between New Jersey and New York. The job gave Vanderbilt a chance to learn about the burgeoning steamship industry. In the late 1820s, he went into business on his own, building steamships and operating ferry lines around the New York region. He had a long and somewhat tumultuous career in steamships and railroads, making many enemies because of his shrewd business practices. When he died at the age of 82 in 1877, he left the bulk of his fortune, estimated at more than $100 million, to his son, William (1821–85).

Vanderbilt borrowed $100 from his mother to start a ferry service across the Hudson River in New York. That ferry service became very profitable. By the time Vanderbilt was done, he had also bought all the rights to the railroads that were shipping goods into New York City. Basically, all the trains had to cross the Hudson River via bridges, and Vanderbilt owned them all. When he died, his net worth was greater than the United States Treasury at that time.[39]

Cornelius had urged that the bulk of the family fortune be endowed upon one descendant, but when Billy died in 1885, he left the family's stake in the company to both of his sons, Cornelius Vanderbilt II and William Kissam Vanderbilt—ignoring his father's wishes. The division of the Vanderbilt fortune in the third generation coincided with a decline in family interest in New York Central and a gradual increase in spending.[40]

Although Billy had doubled his father's fortune over a 15-year period, his decision marked the decline of the Vanderbilt fortune.

By the time the Vanderbilt family had reached the fourth or fifth generation, there were no millionaires left in the Vanderbilt family—none, zero.

Now, contrast that with the Rockefeller family. The Rockefellers, led by John D. Rockefeller, struck it rich in oil. The family fortune was launched in 1858 and, as of 2015, totaled $11 billion. After two centuries, the Rockefeller family is still included on *Forbes*'s list of America's 200 richest families.[41]

Because the Rockefellers put in place certain systems and governance policies among the family members, they have weathered two centuries of economic and social upheavals and maintained their prominence among America's richest families. They can attribute their success to wise guidance, good discipline, smart development, and the proper use and protection of their wealth.

How to Protect Your Family's Wealth Through the Generations

Laura Pitko, whose videos about financial strategies are popular on YouTube, offers an easy-to-understand explanation of why the Rockefellers' legacy continued into perpetuity, while the Vanderbilts' did not.

Pitco says most families' wealth is spent within two generations. An intergenerational wealth system the Rockefellers have used to keep their family wealth intact for five generations is a trust that is run by a Board of Directors. A team of financial professionals called a "family office" manages the family fortune to keep the money in one place, not divided up among family members. This team creates governing documents that specify how the family's fortune can and cannot be spent, based on the values and principles of the person who initiates the trust.[42]

One key element of this strategy is whole life insurance. As Pitko explains in the YouTube video, when a new beneficiary of the family trust is born, the trust can take out a high-cash-value whole life insurance policy for the maximum amount an insurance company will offer on that person. And as soon as a family member and beneficiary dies, the financial team replenishes to the trust any money he or she spent with tax-free funds.

> **You can preserve much more of your hard-earned wealth if you will use whole life insurance to serve as the foundation of your own "family bank."**

Please consult with a knowledgeable financial advisor to execute this strategy in a way that optimizes outcomes for your unique situation.

Chapter 6 Call to Action:

What is the legacy you want to leave? If you have not worked out the details regarding how you want your assets to be distributed and used into perpetuity, discuss this important topic with your family and with your financial advisor.

Special Attention for Closely Held Businesses

Closely held businesses are the backbone of the American enterprise system.

More than 90 percent of all businesses in the United States are closely held corporations. In this type of business, a small group of shareholders controls the firm's operating and managerial policies. (In contrast, in publicly held companies, ownership is widely disbursed, and the firm is administered by professional managers.) Most closely held firms are owned by families.[43]

Closely held businesses often have unique challenges, and often, business owners aren't even aware of those challenges. As a financial advisor, I consider it my duty to let owners of these businesses know about any obstacles that could prevent them from optimizing their outcomes and to offer solutions. Let's look at two common scenarios: business owners who plan to sell their companies and business owners who are in partnerships.

If You Plan to Sell Your Business

Obviously, the strategy you use for your closely held business depends on your plans for the future. For now, let's talk about a situation in which your goal, as a business owner, is ultimately to exit or sell the business. Most people have put so much money and energy into building their businesses that the business becomes a significant part of their net worth.

So when you sell your business, you want to realize its full value. Taxes affect the value of your business, so in essence, one needs $1.67 for every dollar needed to buy a business. In other words, if you were to sell a business for $1, the buyer will have to pay approximately $1.67 because he or she will first have to pay tax on the money made. And if the tax at the state and federal levels is 40 percent on a combined basis, then after the buyer has paid a tax of 40 percent on the $1.67, that person is left with $1 to buy the business.

Now, let's say the person who sold the business built it from his or her own hard work and didn't invest much money in it. Then the $1 he or she receives for that business is subject to capital gains taxation from proceeds of the sale of the business.

As mentioned earlier, a *capital gains tax* is assessed on the difference between the original purchase price of an asset and the price it sells for. Long-term capital gains tax is assessed on the profit from the sale of any asset the owner has held for more than a year. The rates are 0 percent, 15 percent, 20 percent, or 23.8 percent, depending on your tax bracket. Short-term capital gains tax applies to assets held for one year or less and is taxed as ordinary income.[44]

What this means is that of the $1.67 the buyer earned to enable the purchase from the business owner, the state and US government received approximately 90 cents—67 cents from the buyer, plus 23 cents in capital gains tax from the seller. There's something wrong with that math, in my opinion.

I used $1 and $1.67 to simplify the math, but you can add any number of zeros to that calculation because it applies whether it's a $1 million business or a $100 million business.

Our objective is to minimize the amount of money the government gets for the transaction through legal means. Now, this type of solution will not work if you want to sell your business soon—in the next month, for example. However, if you work with your financial advisor in advance of selling your business, you can optimize your outcome by using some financial tools that we have access to as advisors.

If Your Business Is a Partnership

Often, a closely held business is composed of a partnership, and there are multiple owners. In this situation, the business owners are carrying some risks that should be alleviated.

Let's say that two people decide to start a business. To keep the math easy, let's say one puts in $1 million, and the other puts in $1 million. So the business has $2 million in capital. They go to a local bank and tell the banker they are starting ABC business, and they want to get a loan for additional capital in the amount of $4 million each. That would give the business a total initial value of $10 million. As long as things are going fine, that will work out.

What If One Partner Dies or Becomes Disabled?

But now let's say one of the business partners dies prematurely or becomes disabled. Of course that will put a severe strain on the business. If one of the partners dies, the other partner now owns a business that has a $10 million value on paper, and $8 million of that money is from loans. The surviving partner now has to do all the work because the other one is out of the picture. But the partner who died or became disabled still has his or her spouse and children listed as 50 percent stakeholders in the profitability of that business.

Is it fair that one partner is left to do all the work, while the one who is no longer working but remains an owner gets to share half the profits with his or her family? Can the surviving partner get the resources to buy out the other family's business interest?

Businesses like that typically don't have money sitting around in cash; their assets are tied up in inventory, property, equipment, and other things. So one partner might not have $1 million in cash available to buy out the other partner's share of the business from his or her family. So now the surviving partner might go to the bank and say, "Look, my business partner died, and I want to buy his interest out, so I need another $1 million."

Every bank in the country is probably going to tell that person to take a hike. Why? Because now that one of the partners has passed away, the business is a bigger risk to the bank. It no longer has the full function and capabilities that it had when both partners were contributing their expertise and effort to the business. The business isn't likely to be able to generate the kind of profit now that it did when both business partners were working. The business has lost the skill set of the person who has passed away or become disabled.

Second, the business already has the full amount of leverage. The $8 million in loans is still outstanding. Some of the employees may start wondering if they are going to get their next paycheck because one of the founders has passed away. Some of them might become concerned about the future of the business, so they start to look for other employment opportunities. During that process, their productivity declines, which cause the business revenue to suffer. Consequently, there are less profits to share with the surviving spouse of the deceased or disabled owner. And the surviving partner might even have to reduce his or her own take-home compensation.

Adding further insult to all these problems, the obligations to the bank and the interest payments on the loans are still the same. They don't go down just because the business revenue has gone down.

Strategy: A Properly Funded Buy–Sell Agreement

Now, fortunately, we live in a world of solutions, and the solution in this scenario is unbelievably simple: have your team of financial advisors (including a CPA and tax attorney) prepare a buy–sell agreement when you and your partner establish the business.

Such an agreement mandates that, for example, if one of the partners passes away, the surviving partner's family must sell the interest or to the surviving partner, who then must buy out the interest in the business held by the deceased partner's family.

It is important to note, however, that an agreement is no good if it cannot be enforced. You must have the necessary amount of funding behind the agreement, or else it means nothing.

When we talk to most of our clients who are small-business owners, they are not aware of this problem. And if they are aware of it, they don't have a buy–sell agreement in place. And even if they do, often, they don't have the liquidity behind the agreement to enforce it.

Funding is the key!

A life insurance contract can provide the needed funding, either to the business or to the surviving partner so her or she can buy out the decedent's estate

It is important to follow a formula, instead of a dollar amount for the business valuation, because business valuations change over time. Formulas can be tied to profitability, revenue, or an average of the previous two or three years. We can apply the formula to find out the amount of funding that is to be paid to the beneficiaries. As long as the insurance amount is greater than what that formula calculates, there will be enough liquidity for the business or the surviving partner to buy out the decedent's interest.

How to Structure a Buy–Sell Agreement

There are two ways to structure a buy–sell agreement.

One is called an *entity purchase*, where the business owns the life insurance and therefore gets the money to buy out the deceased family's interest. With the second strategy, the surviving partner gets the money as an individual so he or she can buy out the decedents. This is known as a *cross-purchase* agreement.

Usually when you have a small number of partners—perhaps two or three—the latter strategy works because you want to keep that asset on an individual basis rather than at the corporate level. But when you have more than two or three partners, almost always the entity purchase is the better option—having the money go to the business entity.

Either way, a buy–sell agreement funded with appropriate insurance is an excellent way to alleviate this problem. I strongly recommend that you consult an attorney to create this agreement. Although financial advisors can provide you with a sample agreement, you need a legally binding agreement that takes into consideration all the unique aspects of your business and of all owners' personal situations. Most financial advisors do work with legal advisors to ensure an optimized outcome for you.

The Impact to a Business's Balance Sheet when an Owner Dies

The following examples show what happens to a business's balance sheet when a business owner dies. Example 1 shows the "before" and "after" balance sheet impact of the death of an owner when there has been no planning or funding for this contingency. Example 2 shows the "before" and "after" impact when there is proper funding. Clearly with the second situation it is more advantageous to all concerned—Owners, Employees, Bankers, Customers and Family members.

What Happens to a Balance Sheet When a Business Owner Dies?

Example 1

Assumptions:
1. Buy-Sell Agreement, Value $4,800,000 [$2,400,000 each]
2. No Life Insurance to fund agreement

Balance Sheet – Before Death

Assets	
Total Assets	$6,000,000
Liabilities	
Accounts Payable etc.	$2,000,000
Bank Note	750,000
Liabilities	$2,750,000
Stockholder Equity	$3,250,000
Total Liabilities & SH Equity	$6,000,000

Balance Sheet – After Death

Assets	
Total Assets	$6,000,000
Liabilities	
Accounts Payable etc.	$2,000,000
Bank Note	750,000
Note Due to Deceased's Estate	**2,400,000**
Liabilities	$5,150,000
Stockholder Equity	**850,000**
Total Liabilities & SH Equity	$6,000,000

Note: The corporation has booked a new liability: $2,4000,000.
The corporation's book value has gone from $3,250,000 to $850,000.
One key person is dead.

Query: If you were the banker …
1. How much money would you lend this company?
2. Would you release the estate of the deceased from the existing $750,000 note?

Example 2

Assumptions:
1. Buy-Sell Agreement, Value $4,800,000 [$2,400,000 each]
2. Life Insurance of $2,400,000 to fund agreement

Balance Sheet – Immediately Before Death

Assets		Liabilities	
Cash	$2,500,000	Accounts Payable etc.	$2,000,000
Account Receivable	1,500,000	Bank Note	750,000
Fixed Assets	2,000,000	Stockholder Equity	$3,250,000
Total Assets	**$6,000,000**	**Total Liabilities & SH Equity**	**$6,000,000**

Balance Sheet – Immediately After Death

Assets		Liabilities	
Cash	$4,900,000	Accounts Payable etc.	$2,000,000
Account Receivable	1,500,000	Bank Note	750,000
Fixed Assets	2,000,000	Amount Due to Deceased's Estate	2,400,000
Total Assets	**$8,400,000**	Stockholder Equity	3,250,000
		Total Liabilities & SH Equity	**$8,400,000**

Result: The corporation has kept a constant book value of $3,250,000 by funding the agreement. The corporation has purchased the deceased stockholder's interest without incurring a new liability.

Query: Isn't a banker more comfortable lending money to a corporation that has completed the buyout without "booking" a new liability?

Hypothetical example(s) are for illustrative purposes only and are not intended to represent the past or future performance of any specific investment.

It is always good to plan for the "what if" scenarios in a business so you can be prepared in the event that a business owner dies prematurely. If you are a business owner, ask yourself these questions:

- What is the maximum amount of corporate liabilities in our enterprise at any one time in the year?
- Have I, my spouse, or any partners had to back these liabilities with personal guarantees and/or collateral security?
- Are these guarantees joint, and/or are there several?
- Am I aware—and, if applicable, are my spouse and partners aware—of the ramifications of joint and several personal guarantees if one of the guarantors dies or is disabled for the long term?

If not; then these are the only options:

1. Wind up the business.
2. Take in the deceased's family as a "working" partner.
3. Continue to do 100 percent of the work, but split profits with the deceased's family.
4. Hire a replacement, but still split profits with the deceased's family.
5. Buy out the deceased's equity.

Key-Person Insurance

An important concept for owners of closely held businesses to understand is the value of the "key person" who is responsible for that company's success.

How would you feel about buying a business if the person who made the business successful is not there anymore? If you were to buy such a business, how long would it take you to locate and train a new person to do the critical job that makes that business profitable? An important question for business owners is, "Do you have a strategy in place to mitigate or eliminate the risk if you lose one of your key people?" I believe that risk can be easily handled by the use of what we call *golden handcuffs*, also known as *key-person insurance.*

Businesses whose success depends on the talents of one or two people are viewed a higher risk than those in which no single person is indispensable. So how do you mitigate this risk? With key-person life insurance. This type of protection helps potential buyers and lenders become more comfortable with this reality. Generally, a key-person range of coverage is five to ten times the key person's annual compensation.

The loss of the talents of key employees, whether or not they are owners, can financially cripple a company. A key-person insurance contract helps avoid forced liquidation of a business by providing funds to keep the business running during the period of adjustment after such a loss.

Here are seven common uses of key-person coverage:

1. Securing loans for growth
2. Strengthening the business's credit position
3. Providing funds for recruiting and training replacement employees
4. Paying expenses while the business stabilizes
5. Purchasing the business interest from the estate of a deceased owner
6. Salary continuation for a surviving spouse
7. Providing executive compensation arrangements

A popular strategy for accomplishing these goals is to use fully funded flexible life insurance contracts. They offer favorable tax treatment and can be structured to meet various objectives on a selective basis.

If you are establishing an employee incentive and retention plan, you can gain more control over the outcome by taking the following actions:

1. Choose the participants.
2. Choose the funding amounts.
3. Choose the vesting schedules.
4. Choose the age when employees receive their benefits.
5. Leverage the funds for current business needs.
6. Grow the benefits on a tax-deferred basis.
7. Build in a cost-recovery mechanism.
8. Insulate your business from the impact of the death of a key employee.
9. Allow the business to have 100 percent control of access to benefits.
10. Include a non-compete clause.

Would you want to install such a plan? Do you know a financial vehicle that could possibly provide all these benefits? Essentially an Executive Bonus plan using Permanent Life insurance will allow you to cover the following -- Live, Die, Quit and Deduct –for selective employees and be friendly to the business balance sheet. This can also be structured as a "Restrictive Employee Bonus Arrangement" (REBA) by using a vesting schedule.

What if a Key Person Is Uninsurable?

Sometimes, business owners are insurable because of health conditions. To get the life insurance or disability protection anyway, we can still alleviate the tax matter using tax-deferred annuities. For an annuity, you don't have to pay taxes on an annual basis until you withdraw the money. When the employee is fully vested and receives the money, at that time the business gets a tax deduction for the money paid to the employee, and the employee gets a 1099 for the income received.

However, if that employee dies or becomes disabled during the interim period, and there is no coverage, then there is some exposure to the business. The question is, are the business owners willing to assume that risk? And how do they come to a mutually agreed agreement with the employee?

This doesn't happen often, but it has happened.

For instance, in today's day and age, if somebody has tested positive for COVID-19, the insurance company will postpone coverage until the employee tests negative and is no longer a potential risk.

Another example is that if somebody has had a triple-bypass surgery in the past two or three years, many companies would not want to take on that risk. The same is true of someone who has cancer, depending on what stage it is. On the other hand, there is a whole host of issues kind of in-between. For example, a diabetic might not get coverage, but there might be a company that will provide coverage, depending on how high the person's A1C is. Obviously, a diabetic who has no other complications is a better risk, everything else being equal, than somebody who is diabetic and also has high blood pressure, has a family history of heart disease, is overweight, doesn't exercise enough, and is a smoker and a drinker.

We have all kinds of outcomes from an underwriting perspective, but we don't know that until we actually start to deal with a particular situation.

Business owners often have more leverage if they are securing coverage for a group of, say, ten key employees. If two of those ten have some health issues, but the other eight do not, then insurance companies might be a little more liberal in offering key-person coverage. That is less of a risk than covering one key person who has health issues. So we have to look at each individual situation on its own merit.

Deferred Compensation: An Incentive for Key People to Stay on Board

In simple terms, you want to build in a strong incentive for your key people not to quit working for your company. The purpose of "golden handcuffs" is essentially find a way to provide compensation to that key employees in the future—to tie those individuals to the success of the company. You can use vesting formulas and other strategies to accomplish this.

Let's say you are a key employee in my business, and you are making $100,000 per year. And then I tell you, "Because of the wonderful work you've been doing, and we expect you to continue doing for our company, we are going to give you an additional benefit that we don't offer to all the rank-and-file employees." Then I tell you that this benefit is an additional $30,000 per year, on top of your $100,000.

You can invest that money as you please; however, you can't have access to that $30,000 and the accumulation on it for, let's say, ten years. There's no hard and fast rule about this; a business owner can design the benefit in many ways. The idea is to build a time frame that is long enough and consistent enough for the company to get a good return on investment while also serving as a meaningful incentive for the key employee to stay on board.

You can design this incentive so that if the key employee isn't able to finish working for the entire ten-year period, or whatever amount of time it's for, the company will still provide that benefit to the key person's family. You also need to build in a contingency plan in case the key employee leaves the company before those ten years are finished, or if he or she engages in certain acts that are unethical—for example, embezzlement of funds. In those cases, you can fire that employee, and he or she will have to forfeit that money.

You certainly don't expect them to embezzle funds. However, as a business owner, you do not want to assume that risk. A benefit of $30,000 per year for ten years adds up to $300,000. You might not have the liquid resources to come up with that kind of money. So what's the solution? Transfer that risk to an insurance company. Then, if the employee quits before the ten-year period is finished, or if he or she dies or becomes disable, then the insurance company would provide you with that $300,000 amount, or whatever the number is.

Now we return to the topic of taxes. During that ten-year period when the key employee doesn't have access to the $30,000 benefit, which might be growing in value in a stock portfolio, why should your business pay taxes on those gains? It's money that will eventually be paid to the employee anyway. I estimate that 95 percent, and maybe as many as 99 percent, of deferred-compensation strategies like this are funded with life insurance companies because those companies enjoy tax-free or tax-deferred treatment on the money. That eliminates the tax burden associated with the incentive.

Life insurance companies are the only ones that can make a business whole, to honor the terms of your agreement with your employee if you pass away before the ten years are over. In contrast, a bank or investment company will give you only the amount of the account. They will not make up any amount you've lost.

Split-Dollar[45] Allows the Sharing of Cost and Benefit of Permanent Life Insurance

Split-dollar is a strategy that allows the sharing of the cost and benefit of a permanent life insurance policy. Most split-dollar life insurance plans are used in businesses between an employer and employee, or between a corporation and a shareholder. Plans can also be set up between individuals (sometimes called "private split-dollar").

In a split-dollar plan, the two entities draw up a written agreement that outlines how they will share the premium cost, cash value, and death benefit of a permanent life insurance policy.

The following types of business situations could call for the use of "split-dollar" life insurance:

1. Businesses that have or are considering executive deferred compensation plans
2. Business owners with cross-purchase buy–sell agreements.
3. Business owners engaged in estate tax planning with irrevocable trusts
4. Business that will be sold to a key employee
5. C Corporation owners who need personal permanent life insurance
6. Nonprofit organizations interested in incentive compensation plans for executives and directors

Now, let's look at a real-world example of how the split-dollar solution can create an incredibly valuable asset.

How Split-Dollar Agreement Made Coach Jim Harbaugh the Highest-Paid Football Coach in the Country

In August 2016, the University of Michigan announced that it had amended its contract with head football coach Jim Harbaugh to include a creative deferred compensation alternative involving cash value life insurance. The arrangement made Harbaugh the highest paid college football coach in the country, according to *Sports Illustrated* and other news outlets. The compensation strategy was designed to provide Harbaugh with millions of dollars of tax-free cash during retirement.[46]

When Harbaugh was originally hired at Michigan, the parties had agreed to sit down and discuss the establishment of a deferred compensation package after the end of his first season. But instead of a deferred compensation agreement, Harbaugh and Michigan entered into a split-dollar loan agreement, with the university agreeing to make seven loan advances of $2 million each, that Harbaugh would use to pay premiums on a life insurance policy.[47]

As long as the policy remains in force, the loan will not have to be repaid until Harbaugh dies, at which time Michigan will recoup its original $14 million investment, and Harbaugh's beneficiaries will receive the remainder of the death benefit. While some news reports have stated that Harbaugh's beneficiaries are guaranteed to receive at least 150 percent of the amount due back to the University ($21 million, once the full loan has been extended), the actual terms of the loan agreement only require that the residual death benefit (net of the loan) be at least $1,120,000 following Harbaugh's attainment of age 70. Meanwhile, the agreement allows Harbaugh to borrow money from the policy tax-free as long as the policy continues to meet certain sustainability requirements immediately following the loan.[48]

No bank loan can match that type of leverage!

The Importance of a Business Valuation

A 409A valuation is an appraisal of the fair-market value of a private company's common stock. With publicly traded stock, we can easily see the specific prices for any company, but private companies need an independent valuation to see how much their company stock is worth.

The law requires companies to get a 409A valuation to ensure that your stock options are not undervalued. Undervaluing stock options can result in major IRS penalties and lost compensation. If you plan to offer common stock options, then you must get a 409A valuation every twelve months and any time your company closes a new funding round.[49]

Section 409A was added to the IRS code as part of the American Jobs Creation Act of 2004. It states, "Section 409A applies to compensation that workers earn in one year, but that is paid in a future year. This is referred to as nonqualified deferred compensation." This is different from deferred compensation in the form of elective deferrals to qualified plans [such as a 401(k) plan, a 403(b) plan, or a 457(b) plan.] Stock options are considered deferred compensation. A 409A valuation will determine a 'strike price' (the price at which your employees can buy equity in your company) that must be at or above fair-market value."

Small and intermediate-sized nonprofits that want to retain their chief rainmakers who bring in the majority of donations need an alternative to traditional deferred-compensation plans that fall outside the scope of Section 409A. They need a solution that enables them to compete for, and retain personnel with, large corporations with nonqualified executive benefits budgets. The ability to create such a program may be found within Section 409A itself.[50]

One strategy is the "short-term deferral" (Section 409A, Reg. 1.409A-l(b)(4)) exception which, when combined with an endorsement split-dollar plan, has the potential to be a very lucrative benefit with strings attached. The "short-term deferral" exception refers to the timing of the distribution of plan assets upon plan termination. That is the key to escaping the Section 409A umbrella. The employee must receive the policy used in the split-dollar arrangement within 2.5 months of the end of the corporate tax year in which the service requirement was completed (for twenty years, at age sixty-five, etc.). This rule has to be adhered to strictly but, as long as it is, Section 409A does not apply.[51]

The owners of closely held businesses would be wise to consult with a team of financial experts to try to anticipate every potential roadblock to business optimization, including taxes and other issues. The ideal time to discuss these issues is when you are in the planning stages of establishing a business, with regular conversations taking place to make sure you are continuing to optimize your outcomes as your business grows.

Chapter 7 Call to Action:

To protect the future of your business in the event that one owner dies or becomes disabled, have your team of financial advisors (including a CPA and a tax attorney) prepare a buy–sell agreement when you and your partner(s) establish the business.

Sound Strategies for Small Nonprofits

In my firm, we work with a lot of small nonprofits, and they have unique financial needs. This is not an official definition, but I consider a nonprofit to be small if it has an annual budget of $2 million or less. Typically, small nonprofits are not national; they are local or regional.

Small nonprofits tend to struggle with similar issues. It is rewarding when my team and I design solutions that alleviate those issues for the leaders of those organizations. Here are some recommendations that can help nonprofit boards ensure the long-term stability of their organizations.

Charitable Lead Trusts

Given historically low interest rates, a popular approach has been to encourage donors to establish charitable lead trusts (CLT), which in effect enable a large income tax deduction to the grantor for the current year by bringing forward the present value of future gifts and allowing the grantor to receive the remainder interest. This enables a consistency of donations to the charity for an extended duration of time.

Here is an example of a CLT established recently:

- A 5 percent grantor lead annuity trust for a charity for 20 years
- Principal of $1 million
- IRS discount rate of 3 percent;
- Income tax deduction is $743,000
- $50,000 is provided annually to the charity for 20 years; the remainder value in trust comes back to the donor or other beneficiaries at the end of the term.

Please note while the donor receives an income tax deduction up front for the present value of the future distributions to charity, the donor does *not* receive any additional income tax deductions for distributions made to charities over the term of the trust. Keep in mind, even though the donor's assets have been transferred into the grantor CLT, they continue to function as if they are still the property of the donor throughout the operation of the trust. This means that the income earned from those assets is treated as the donor's income over the years of the trust. Also, any capital gains realized in the trust are treated as if they were realized by the donor; hence, the donor of a grantor charitable lead trust is taxed on both the income earned in the trust and the capital gains realized in the trust for each calendar year.

Here is a diagram showing the concept:

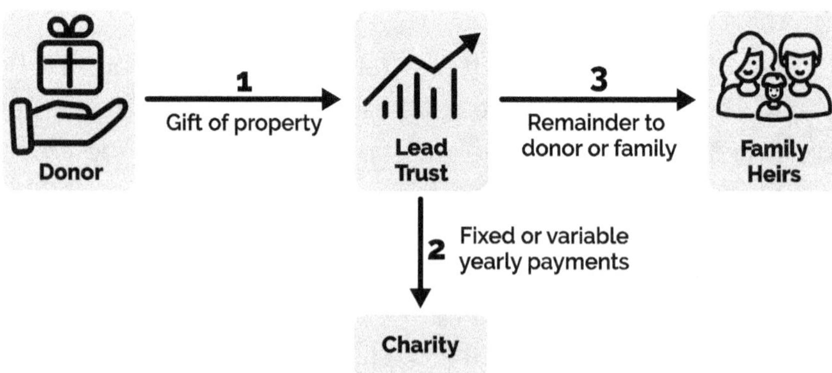

Establish an Endowment

A lot of smaller nonprofits, in my opinion, struggle with budgets and fund-raising, pretty much on an annual basis, because many of them lack an endowment. Larger, national nonprofits such as the United Way and Rotary International have large operating budgets of millions of dollars. They can fund their programs on an annual basis from the earnings of their endowments.

I have found that leaders of small nonprofits either aren't aware that they need to start an endowment, or they put off the task of starting one. In the latter case, even if nonprofit leaders are aware of the value of an endowment, they tend to think it's more important to fund *current* expenditures rather than it is to put money aside in an endowment that will be beneficial to them in the long term.

> Most charities struggle because they
> do not have an endowment.

My thoughts on this topic are similar to those I have about planning for individuals—if we try hard enough, most of us can live on 90 percent of all we earn. If we can encourage the leaders of small nonprofits to set aside 10 cents of every dollar they bring in, then after a few years, that money will provide its own earnings and interest. Then, from that point forward, the stress of raising money is somewhat reduced.

Here is an example. Let's say a nonprofit has an annual budget of $1 million. In the absence of changing their policy, they would have to raise $1 million every year to meet their obligations for their programs. In a situation like the Coronavirus, or Covid-19 pandemic, nonprofits are struggling because they cannot go about their business as they normally would. Perhaps the individuals and organization that support them cannot continue to do so because they, too, are suffering financially. Plus, nonprofits are unable to hold the public fund-raising events they are accustomed to hosting because of state governments' stay-at-home mandates.

So this nonprofit is unable to raise the $1 million it needs to operate its annual budget for the next year. But what if we could go to the board of directors and suggest a different way of doing things? The suggestion is to set aside 10 percent of the current year's $1 million budget—$100,000—in an endowment fund and then continue to do that every year for a few years. After five years, there will be about $500,000 in that account, ignoring any earnings and investment return. Let's say the earnings on that amount of $500,000, at 5 percent interest, total $25,000 per year.

In this hypothetical example, starting in year six, the nonprofit has to raise only $975,000 for its yearly operating budget, instead of $1 million, because it is getting $25,000 in earnings from the endowment.

The endowment, in effect, distributes those earnings to the operating side of that nonprofit. In the long run, the endowment will provide even more benefit to the organization. To accomplish this, the leaders must take a long-term view.

Rotary International's Endowment

One of the largest endowments in the world is that of the Rotary International Foundation. (Rotary International is an international service organization that was established in Chicago in 1905.) The very first deposit to start that endowment, a little more than one hundred years ago, was a mere $26.50. Today, that endowment is valued at several billion dollars. Every year, the Rotary organization distributes approximately $100 million to qualified charities around the world.

I realize that's an example of a large nonprofit, but the point is that the endowment started out extremely small. Because the board and members contributed to it every year, the fund grew significantly.

How an Endowment Works

Let's say I support a nonprofit whose mission I really believe in. I give the organization $10,000 each year. Over time, the nonprofit becomes reliant on my continuing to give it $10,000. Now, I am probably not the only person donating money to the nonprofit; others are donating various amounts as well. Let's say this nonprofit has a program that educates underprivileged girls around the world—a cause I am passionate about. That school becomes dependent on my ability to continue providing it with $10,000 each year.

What happens when I pass away? Well, my kids and grandkids most likely will not have the same degree of affinity and fondness for that nonprofit and its program that I do, so they probably will not continue supporting it. As a result, my $10,000-per-year contribution will dry up.

The question that should be asked is this: If a cause is important enough for me to support during my lifetime, why is it not important to ensure that continued support when I'm dead and gone? The next question is, how do I continue to support that organization after I am gone?

The solution is quite simple. I recommend that small nonprofits review their list of donors—the people who are providing support— and see which one of the major donors might be willing to perpetuate their support by, for example, naming the nonprofit as a beneficiary of their estate plans or retirement plans, or by establishing a bequest.

These are great ways to ensure the long-term viability of a nonprofit using its existing donor pool.

Charitable Remainder Trust with risk transfer to an Insurance Company

Now, let's say I give that nonprofit $500,000, and I ask its leaders to give me 5 percent of that amount each year, or $25,000, for the rest of my life. Then, when I die, they can have the amount that's left in the fund. In other words, the charity has the remainder interest, and I have the income interest during lifetime.

On one hand, the nonprofit is glad to receive my $500,000 donation but, uncertainty abounds. This is because:

- The gift is realized only if a balance remains upon my death.
- The nonprofit is solely responsible for making lifetime payments to me.
- Sufficient reserves must be maintained to back these annuity payments.
- The nonprofit must maintain charitable investment pools (when there are multiple donors) with ongoing management fees.

Effectively, by accepting that money, the organization has a liability to me for the rest of my life, in the amount of $25,000 per year. They don't know how long I'm going to live. Therefore, they cannot use my donation of $500,000 in its entirety. If they did, they would effectively be taking a risk that if I lived a very, very long time, they are out *more than* the $500,000.

So, how can we meet the obligation and the liability to the donor while providing this bequest while also being budget-friendly to the nonprofit? The answer is that we *shift the risk to an insurance company.* The way this solution works will depend on interest rates and the donor's age but will generally provide the following assurances:

- The cash is freed up for immediate use by the nonprofit while the donor is living.
- Payments to a donor are guaranteed by a highly regulated insurance company.
- Uncertainty about investments and donors' life expectancy are gone because the risks are assumed by the insurance company.
- Most commercial annuity contracts have no recurring management fees.

Let's say I am the nonprofit's financial advisor, and I advise its board that I will seek out insurance companies that will give a contractual promise to the donor that he or she will receive $25,000 per year for the rest of his or her life. I will find out how much the insurance company needs in order to deliver that $25,000 per year for the rest of the donor's life.

Now, let's say the donor is 70 years old, and the interest rate is 5 percent. The insurance company tells me that its best offer is that it will accept $350,000 and take on the obligation to provide $25,000 a year to the donor, no matter how long he lives. Assuming the nonprofit board accepts this offer to transfer the risk to the insurance company, what are the board members left with? They are left with $150,000 that they can use right away, without being stressed about the terms of the agreement with the donor because the insurance company will provide the $25,000 to him annually.

Consider an Annuity

To enable the nonprofit to use some of those funds sooner rather than actually holding a liability on its balance sheet, they could use a commercial annuity from the insurer to meet both objectives. This also effectively transfers all the investment and longevity risk to the insurer. The diagram below shows the concept.

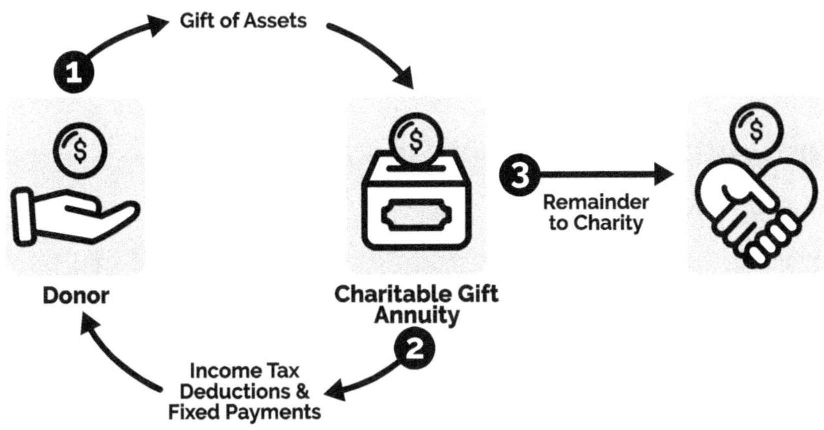

Secure Key-Person Insurance

Usually, when a small nonprofit is established, there are one or two founders who are the visionaries—the people who essentially run the show. Yes, they end up establishing a board of directors eventually, but for the most part, the nonprofit's success depends on the reputation of these visionaries. As these leaders age, it is possible that their initial degree of effort and enthusiasm will wane.

In such situations, to provide continuity for the nonprofit and its board, we believe it is essential for the leaders to secure key-person insurance. We discussed this important coverage in chapter 7, but it is also an important resource in the nonprofit world. If a leader, or key person, of the nonprofit passes away, this insurance ensures that there is an infusion of capital into the nonprofit that will allow it to have the resources to groom somebody who can take over the leadership of the organization.

The board might choose to groom somebody internally, or they might go out and recruit someone via a head-hunting firm. That takes money. So, instead of taking dollars away from the nonprofit's annual programs, that money comes from key-person insurance, if it was secured in advance of the person's death.

Small nonprofits need a lifeline in such situations more than large nonprofits do. They must not overlook the need for key-person insurance. Again, this solution requires a focus on the organization's long-term stability.

Work with a Competent Financial Advisor

In 2017, the tax rates were reduced for individuals and businesses, but not for trusts. This means that if a trust is formed that has an income generation of greater than $15,000, it is subject to the highest rate of taxation for an individual, which is the rate assessed to people who earn more than $600,000 per year.

Why does this matter? Because many nonprofits' donations are tied to a taxable income and/or ability to take deductions. In such a case, I recommend that they consider changing the underlying investment vehicle that is generating the taxable income in a way that reduces, eliminates or postpones the taxes.

Too often, I find that small nonprofits and charities are not doing a deep enough dive into their financial situations. Many times, it's because they simply don't have the staff and other resources to devote to this effort. Many of these organizations are run by volunteers who are not necessarily professionals and often do not have the resources of hiring the advisor as an employee or otherwise willing to engage him or her to look into all these financial options each year.

When they receive this specialized service from a competent third-party advisor, I believe it will provide the nonprofit boards and their donors with greater confidence. A lot of times, when people give money to nonprofits and charities, they are concerned that they don't know how much of that money is going toward the true purpose and how much is being squandered in administrative efforts. Donors want to make sure the nonprofit's overhead is reasonable. They want to make sure the money is appropriately invested, not misused. They want to make sure it's monitored. They want to make sure the books are up-to-date. The more transparency there is, the more the nonprofit organization can ensure compliance with that qualified outside third party rather than somebody on the board, who could potentially have a conflict of interest. This strategy is better for that organization on a longer-term basis.

It has been our experience, though, that it is not easy to get people to think about their nonprofits' long-term stability because these solutions require majority approval of the board to proceed. As financial advisors, we often have to present these solutions to nonprofit board members several times. Hopefully, as we continue advising them over time, they will see the value in our recommendations. Just like the Rotary International endowment, a small endowment can grow to be significant. But we have to start somewhere; we have to plant the seeds and initiate those discussions.

Chapter 8 Call to Action:

If you manage a nonprofit, work with your financial advisor and other financial experts to establish an endowment that will distribute earnings to the operating side of your nonprofit and secure key-person insurance for the leaders of your nonprofit.

Whom to Hire and Whom to Inform

> "While good advice doesn't have to be
> expensive, bad advice will almost always
> cost you dearly, no matter how little
> you pay for it."
>
> —Larry Swedroe, Director of Research,
> Buckingham Asset Management

In chapter 8, I stressed the importance of finding a competent financial advisor to provide guidance to nonprofit board members as they guide their organizations into the future. This advice is wise for everyone—individuals, business owners, and CEOs.

There are many financial advisors to choose from. So in this chapter, I offer my recommendations for screening and selecting an advisor who will guide you as you plan for the future and optimize the value you get from your hard-earned money. Tips for selecting a financial advisor composes the "whom to hire" portion of this chapter.

Then, once you have your financial house in order, it is extremely important that you inform your loved ones about the planning you have done. Tips in this area compose the "whom to inform" part of this chapter.

When you enter an ongoing advice relationship with a financial advisor, you benefit from everything the advisor offers—education, credentials, wisdom, knowledge, discipline, etc.

How Financial Advisors Provide Value

The goal of most reputable financial advisors is to far exceed in deliverable value to their clients what they ever receive in fees from them. Consider that most advisors will do the following for clients—and look for one who will work with you to:

- Develop financial goals.
- Create a timeline.
- Understand risk tolerance and expected rate of return.
- Use data to analyze existing investments, and make recommendations about what to do going forward.
- Determine your optimum asset mix.
- Create a plan for retirement.
- Understand and communicate risks.
- Estimate your expected rate of return.
- Help decide which investments to own in non-retirement accounts.
- Look for ways to reduce taxable income.
- Understand taxes that you incur when you buy or sell investments.
- Identify how much you need to save.
- Provide access to many types of retirement accounts to use (IRA, ROTH, 401(k), 403(b), Defined Benefit, etc).
- Understand the types of insurance and how much you need (including life, long-term care, disability, health, and property & casualty).
- Manage an emergency fund.
- Explore what changes might improve your tax situation.

- Discuss leasing vs. buying.
- Mortgage refinancing, including reverse mortgages.
- Optimize your cash management.
- Explore commercial financing/lending.
- Evaluate vacation property.
- Develop charitable bequest strategies.
- Create business exit strategies.
- Work with your other professional advisors.

Ask People You Trust for References

Chances are, you have asked people you know and trust for referrals to competent, reliable professionals for everything from car repair to home maintenance to medical care. This is a good place to start when searching for a financial advisor as well.

If you have found an advisor you are considering but don't know much about, ask him or her to provide you with references from clients they have worked with. Contact those clients and pick their brains about what they like about the advisor and what they don't like.

Just like you test-drive a car before you buy it, or you walk through a home you are thinking about buying, you should meet with a few potential advisors. Now, it isn't necessary to meet with forty different advisors, but meet with at least two or three. Compare their philosophies, their processes, how comfortable you feel with them, their fee structure, and other criteria. Then proceed with the one who seems to be ideally suited to your situation. Keep in mind that you can always change advisors if the one you choose doesn't work out for some reason.

In fact, if you already have a financial advisor, it doesn't hurt to get a second opinion on matters of significant importance. After all, no one person or firm has a patent on all the good ideas in the business.

> **Do you have enough confidence in your current advisor to get a second opinion?**

Review advisors objectively. Avoid choosing an advisor just because he or she contacted you via a marketing campaign. And if you meet someone socially who mentions that he or she is a financial advisor, review that person's credentials just as you would any other advisor's. This will help you eliminate advisors who probably aren't ideal for you and move forward with those you should consider working with.

Choose an Advisor with Experience or One Who Works with a Team

I recommend that you work with an advisor who has been in the business for at least three or four years. Generally, longer tenure in the career is better because that means the advisor has navigated clients through different business cycles, economic cycles, market fluctuations, and clients' changing situations.

Now, this does not mean that somebody who's young and new to the advisory profession cannot have clients. I value and appreciate the young advisors who are entering this profession. Our industry needs an infusion of young talent. If you are thinking about working with a newer advisor, consider choosing one who works as part of a team of advisors who are more experienced. Many firms believe strongly in the team approach because there is great synergy when advisors who each have expertise in a certain area pool their talents to serve clients and ensure that their best interests are met.

Work with an Independent Advisor

Everything else being equal, I recommend that you work with an advisor who works on an independent basis and is not beholden to a particular financial institution.

This does not mean that all the advisors working for a particular company are not qualified. It does mean that they might be limited to offering only that company's proprietary services and products. An independent advisor, in most cases, can offer you a wider array of options.

Work with an Advisor Who Has Credentials

The insurance and financial services industry is heavily regulated and involves complex financial solutions in the form of various products and services. When seeking a financial advisor to work with, choose one who has earned designations in the specialty areas that relate to your financial situation. As you interview potential advisors, what are their credentials beyond just the licenses that are required to be in this business?

When you see abbreviations after an advisor's name, they don't mean much until you know what those letters stand for. The following is a list of just a few of the many credentials that agents and advisors can earn:

Abbreviation of Designation	Name of Designation	About the Designation
AAI	Accredited Adviser in Insurance	Earned by insurance producers who demonstrate superior knowledge of their field compared to average agents. Insurance professionals earn the title by passing a series of three tests administered by the Insurance Institute of America.
AAMS®	Accredited Asset Management Specialist™	Provides advisors with a strong fundamental financial knowledge with a specific focus on asset management and investments.

Abbreviation of Designation	Name of Designation	About the Designation
ADPA®	Accredited Domestic Partnership Advisor™	Encompasses wealth transfers, federal taxation, retirement planning, and planning for financial and medical end-of-life needs for domestic partners. Individuals must pass an end-of-course examination that tests their ability to synthesize complex concepts and apply theoretical concepts to real-life situations.
AEP®	Accredited Estate Planner	A graduate-level specialization in estate planning, obtained in addition to already recognized professional credentials within the various disciplines of estate planning.
AFA®	Accredited Financial Analyst	Focuses on the global markets and analysis and prepares the professional to understand financial statements and to analyze financial, legal, and economic data.
AFC®	Accredited Financial Counselor®	Indicates that a professional can educate clients on financial principles, assist them with paying off debt, help identify and change poor money-management habits, and support them as they work through financial challenges.
AIF®	Accredited Investment Fiduciary®	Focuses on ethical behavior, fiduciary services, and improving client service. Advisors with this designation have learned to balance their business interests against a client-first (or fiduciary) approach.

Abbreviation of Designation	Name of Designation	About the Designation
CAIA	Chartered Alternative Investment Analyst	Indicates professionals who have met an educational standard for specialists in the area of alternative investments, including hedge funds, venture capital, private equity, funds of funds, derivatives, and real estate investments.
CEBS	Certified Employee Benefit Specialist®	Indicates a financial professional specializing in employer-sponsored retirement plans.
CFA®	Chartered Financial Analyst®	A post-graduate professional qualification offered internationally by the American-based CFA Institute to investment and financial professionals. It has the highest level of global legal and regulatory recognition of finance-related qualifications.
CFP®	Certified Financial Planner™	Provides extensive training and experience, and requires professionals to commit to the CFP Board's ethical standards that require them to put their clients' interests first (i.e., to be fiduciaries).
ChFC®	Chartered Financial Consultant®	Covers a must-have list of requirements for financial advisors, from knowledge on tax and retirement planning to special-needs advising, wealth management, insurance, and more.

Abbreviation of Designation	Name of Designation	About the Designation
CIC	Chartered Investment Counselor	Provides agents/advisors with practical and real-world education that will help them become successful. The program is for full-time agents, brokers, underwriters, etc., who have at least two years of full-time experience in the insurance industry.
CLU®	Chartered Life Underwriter®	Gives advisors in-depth knowledge of life insurance underwriting concepts and life insurance law within the context of overall risk management, the necessary knowledge to help clients address their estate-planning needs, and an understanding of solutions addressing the life insurance underwriting needs of business owners and professionals.
CMA	Certified Management Accountant	Qualifies those who hold it to work in corporate financial accounting and strategic management settings. Professionals often choose this pathway because it covers topics not included in the CPA certification, such as management and executive-level duties.

Abbreviation of Designation	Name of Designation	About the Designation
CPA	Certified Public Accountant	The respected mark of excellence for public accountants. Requirements for the CPA are set by each state board of accountancy. The requirements include completing a program of accounting study at a college or university, passing the Uniform CPA Exam, and meeting experience requirements. Most states require at least a bachelor's degree to become a CPA.
CPCU®	Chartered Property Casualty Underwriter	Earned by individuals who specialize in risk management and property & casualty insurance. Provides professionals with in-depth information on risk-management principles, as well as complex policy and coverage analysis.
FRM®	Financial Risk Manager	Viewed as the globally recognized gold standard for risk professionals. Teaches how to better identify and allocate potential risks, mitigate them, provide recommendations for better decisions in regard to all risks, and make a risk-management plan. Helps professionals improve how to prioritize risks, ensure they are aggressively and cost-effectively managed, and provide directions and recommendations on issues that are critical for success.

Abbreviation of Designation	Name of Designation	About the Designation
LIFA	Licensed International Financial Analyst	Designed for investment professionals worldwide to help them attain higher levels of professionalism and ethics in the global industry of investment management and analysis. The examinations require an in-depth knowledge of investment principles, along with an understanding of global capital markets.
LUTCF®	Life Underwriter Training Council Fellow	Often considered the first designation any insurance professional should earn. Integrates four practice specialties: life insurance and annuities, health and employee benefits, multiline, and financial advising and investments.

Work with an Advisor Who Is Active in the Industry

Being active in industry organizations is certainly not mandatory. However, financial advisors who serve in leadership roles in industry organizations are most likely well connected to many other professionals in the industry. A few of the well-known organizations are the Financial Planning Association (FPA), the Financial Services Institute (FSI), the National Association of Insurance and Financial Advisors (NAIFA), the National Association of Professional Financial Advisors (NAPFA), and the Society of Financial Service Professionals (SFSP) and the Million Dollar Round Table (MDRT).

Work with an Advisor Who Is Willing to Work with Your Other Experts

As you talk with advisors you are considering working with, ask them how willing they are to work with the other experts you have relied on in the past, such as your CPA, your trust officer, and/or your estate-planning attorney. Most advisors are happy to do so, but don't assume they do. Ask the question.

If you do not have a relationship with these professionals, ask advisors you are interviewing if they do. They will probably be happy to refer you to these important members of the advisory team to ensure that all your financial and related needs are covered and your best interests are the focus.

> The best interest of the client is the only interest to be considered.

Share Key Elements of Your Financial Situation with Your Beneficiaries

Now that we have discussed "whom to hire," let's discuss "whom to inform."

If you expend the time, effort, and money creating a financial plan, an estate plan, a will, a trust, and other important documents, but you fail to inform your beneficiaries about them, your situation is not likely to be optimized. The advisor you work with will be a tremendous help in this area. He or she will collect the names and contact information of everyone who needs to know details about your financial situation in case of an emergency.

I have found it helpful to conduct family meetings with my clients and their children, grandchildren, and other people who the clients want to inform about the financial plans and documents they have put in place. Some people are sensitive about their finances and prefer to keep these details confidential. But I think it is important to share at least the big picture with loved ones so that if the client becomes incapacitated or passes away, the next generation needs to get involved. Having important information documented in writing, or perhaps on a video, will help the client's family navigate the complex area of asset transfer. Survivors will appreciate having a smooth transition during a difficult time.

It is important to keep these documents up-to-date. Too many times, people get all their documents in order but then fail to update them after a business splits up or a couple divorces. Having a knowledgeable, competent financial advisor on your team helps you ensure that your documents are always up-to-date and that they reflect your current situation.

I firmly believe that if there is a split in the family or a split in the business, an advisor should work with only one side, for one person or business. If a couple or business retained an advisor for many years but then a split occurs, that advisor needs to work with only one party, and the other party should seek out a different advisor.

Chapter 9 Call to Action:

Select a qualified, competent financial advisor you can trust and work with for the long term to optimize your financial outcome. Ask people you know and trust for referrals, and then interview several. Once you and your advisor have developed a financial plan to optimize your future, inform your beneficiaries about these documents, and share your advisor's contact information with them.

Bringing It Back Full Circle into Perpetuity

> "All I want in life is an unfair advantage."
>
> —Hank Greenberg

I would like to complement you on completing the process of digesting the material in this book. I hope you realize the value in engaging a competent financial advisor.

According to a 2019 survey, only 17 percent of Americans work with a financial advisor.[52] This is unfortunate because advisors can help you optimize outcomes and instill in your future generations the values and principles that can perpetuate the well-being of families, communities, and indeed the country so that there is less need for government subsidies as people become more self-reliant.

As an industry, we know this works, based on the concept of "the aggregation of marginal gains" applied over the long term, as eloquently captured in the book *Atomic Habits* by James Clear. Properly customizing the programs outlined in this book to your unique situation will give you the proper coordinates for the **GPS** of your assets:

- **G**row assets
- **P**ass on assets
- **S**pend assets

If you found even one concept or idea herein worth sharing, please pass this book along to a colleague, family member, friend, or even other advisors who could benefit from learning more about holistic wealth creation, preservation, and management. Sharing this information will help bring sound financial strategies full circle into perpetuity.

Action items you will take:

1. ____

2. ____

3. ____

4. ____

5. ____

6. ____

7. ____

8. ____

9. ____

10. ____

Glossary of Terms

Accumulation phase of retirement—The years during which you are working and saving money to fund your retirement

Annuity—A series of payments made at equal intervals

Asset diversification—The process of investing in a variety of assets in an attempt to reduce the exposure to any one particular asset or risk and to reduce risk or volatility

Backdoor Roth IRA—An informal name for a complicated, IRS-sanctioned method for high-income taxpayers to fund a Roth, even if their income is higher than the maximum the IRS allows for regular Roth contributions

Bond—A fixed-income instrument that represents a loan made by an investor to a borrower (typically corporate or governmental), used by companies, municipalities, states, and sovereign governments to finance projects and operations

Buy–sell agreement—A legally binding contract that stipulates how a business partner's share of a business may be reassigned if that partner dies or leaves the business

Capital gains tax—A levy assessed on the positive difference between the sale price of an asset and its original purchase price.

Deferred compensation—A portion of an employee's compensation that is set aside to be paid at a later date

Disability waiver premium option—An option that waives your premium but keeps your insurance policy in force as long as you, the insured, are disabled

Discretionary income—The amount of your income that is left for spending, investing, or saving after you pay taxes and pay for personal necessities, such as food, shelter, and clothing

Distribution phase of retirement—The years during which you are no longer working in a full-time job and during which you are withdrawing money from your retirement account(s)

Dollar-cost averaging—A popular strategy you can use during the accumulation phase of retirement to reduce the cost of acquiring investments

Endowment—A donation of money or property to a nonprofit organization, which uses the resulting investment income for a specific purpose

Equities—The same as stocks, which are shares in a company. If you buy stocks, you are buying and are a partial owner of shares in a company

Estate tax—A levy on estates whose value exceeds an exclusion limit set by law

Fixed annuity—An insurance contract that guarantees that the insurer will pay the purchaser a guaranteed, fixed interest rate on his or her contributions to the annuity for a specific period of time.

Fixed expense—An expense that is the same from one month to the next, such as a mortgage payment

Guaranteed insurability option—An option that allows you to increase your coverage in the future, regardless of what your health might be. You can use this option to buy more coverage without having to undergo medical exams or underwriting.

Key-person insurance—Life insurance on people in a business who play key roles; this coverage is typically five to ten times the key person's annual compensation.

Long-term-care rider—An attachment to a permanent life insurance policy that accelerates the death benefit to help pay for the costs of long-term-care services if you become chronically ill

Overloan protection rider—An option that protects you from a situation in which you take money out of your policy for living benefits or to put a down payment on a home or start a business, and your collateral fluctuates in value. Essentially, this rider freezes policies where loan balances exceed a certain threshold as a percentage of cash value in the policy.

Permanent insurance—An umbrella term for life insurance

policies that do not expire

Stocks—A type of security that gives stockholders a share of ownership in a company

Tax-deferred—No tax is due now, but it will be due once you withdraw the funds in retirement

Tax diversification—Having some money in accounts that are taxed now but will be tax-free later; some money in accounts that are tax-deferred and some tax free

Term life insurance—Life insurance for a specified duration, such as 30 years. If you die during that designated period, then the insurance company will pay a benefit to your beneficiaries. But if you outlive that term, then you no longer have life insurance.

Variable expense—An expense that varies from month to month, such as a utility bill

What I Believe

Many aspects of life, and of financial planning, are uncertain. However, throughout my career, I have come to believe steadfastly in certain truths that apply both to advisors/agents and to consumers/investors. Some of those truths are sprinkled throughout the book; here are additional truths for you to consider.

1. The biggest fish are in the roughest waters.
2. In real estate investing, the four most important factors are the deal, the tenant, the location, and the financing.
3. You cannot outgive God.
4. You are already a philanthropist. The only question is this: Is it voluntary (charity) or involuntary (IRS)?
5. For optimal estate planning: "Don't own anything, but control everything." —Simon Singer
6. Risk is always equal to historical volatility.
7. The financial planning paradox: complexity of choice drives down optimization and promotes inertia.
8. Pre-retirees and the retired need to ask themselves this question: "What do I want my money to do while I am alive? What do I want my money to do when I die?" Remember the number of days *to* retirement is known, but the number of days *in* retirement is unknown.
9. Money does not come with instructions.
10. "An asset is something that puts money into your pocket, and a liability is something that takes money out of your pocket." —Robert Kiyosaki, author of *Rich Dad, Poor Dad*

11. "There is no information in past returns of three to five years. That's just noise! It really takes very long periods of time, and it takes a lot of stick-to-it-iveness. You have to really decide what your strategy is based on—long period of returns—and then stick to it." —Eugene Fama

12. In lotteries, you need a dollar and a dream; with equities, you need a dollar and a consistent investment plan.

13. "I like the dreams of the future better than the history of the past." —Thomas Jefferson

14. "When there is blood on the street, I am buying." —Baron Rothschild

15. "Be moderate in order to taste the joys of life in abundance."— Epicurus

16. Shouldn't the rest of your life be the best of your life?

17. Sometimes in life, we get a chance for a "do over," known as a *mulligan* in golf. We have recently seen that with the opportunities presented in the market pullback due to COVID-19 for the benefit of those who might have missed out in Y2K or the 2008–09 recession in terms of investing on the lows. However, we have to "get death right" because there are no do-overs or mulligans. There is exactly one chance to get it right.

18. The reality is that The Final Act could occur at any time. There is no season for death. We all think about living well, so why not think about dying well?

19. Pretend you are directing the movie of your life. How do you want the story to end?

20. "While nothing is more uncertain than the duration of a single life, there is nothing more certain than the average duration of a thousand lives." —Elizur Wright, American mathematician known as the Father of Life Insurance

21. "If you could remove the government from your retirement plan; how quickly do you want to get started?" —John Wheeler

22. "One way or another, you are going to leave a legacy. We can either set it up now and define the legacy, or you can let your kids, the government, or a nursing home define it. Write your own playbook—don't let someone else." —Joseph Spinelli

23. Without planning, the following language is required to be included in all family business agreements: "Upon the transfer of ownership (death or gifts), except for transfers to a spouse with the same rights the owner held prior to the transfer, the owner's uncle shall have an unqualified right to receive 40 percent of the value of the business over $10 million (plus indexing for inflation). Such amounts shall be paid to the uncle in cash within nine months. This right will have priority over any other right of any other owner." That "uncle" is Uncle Sam, the government. This is why proper planning is imperative for optimizing your outcome.

24. Before retirement, your time horizon is known; after retirement, your time horizon is unknown.

25. Every dollar has a job. The goal of planning is to clarify the job for each of your dollars and then identify the most efficient way to get the job done.

26. People know how much money they have, but many don't have a good idea what they can expect from that money.

27. "A margin of safety is achieved when securities are purchased at prices sufficiently below underlying value to allow for human error, bad luck, or extreme volatility in a complex, unpredictable and rapidly changing world."—Seth Klarman, *Margin of Safety*, 1991

28. "Practically speaking, retirees in their seventies and eighties who are interested in acquiring a life annuity but are waiting for interest rates to improve might be surprised to learn that interest rates increasing by a percentage point or two will not make much difference in their income. For people in their seventies and eighties, mortality rates are what drive payouts." —Professor Moshe Milevsky

Recommended Reading

1. *The Value of Debt* by Thomas J. Anderson
2. *Ten Global Trends* by Ronald Bailey and Marian Tupy
3. *The New Life insurance Investment Advisor* by Ben G. Baldwin
4. *Confessions of a CPA* by Brian S. Bloom, CPA
5. *The Millionaire Booklet* by Grant Cardone
6. *Mistakes Millionaires Make* by Harry Clark
7. *Atomic Habits* by James Clear
8. *7 Habits of Highly Effective People* by Stephen Covey
9. *Don't be caught Dead* by William Culp, Jr. JD, LLM, CPA
10. *Guaranteed Income* by Barry James Dyke
11. *The 702(j) Retirement Plan* by Tom Dyson
12. *The Number* by Lee Eisenberg
13. *Paychecks for Life* by Charles D. Epstein
14. *Everything Is Possible* by Mehdi Fakharzadeh
15. *Nothing Is Impossible* by Mehdi Fakharzadeh
16. *10 Most Expensive Tax Mistakes* by Rao K. Garuda, ChFC, CLU
17. *The E-Myth* by Michael Gerber
18. *Rescuing Retirement* by Teresa Ghilarducci & Tony James
19. *The Conversation* by Harley Gordon
20. *Paychecks and Playchecks* by Tom Hegna
21. *Happy Money* by Ken Honda

50. *The Retirement Savings Time Bomb* by Ed Slott, CPA

51. *Expensive Mistakes when Buying and Selling Companies* by Richard Steiglitz, PhD

52. *Goals* by Brian Tracy

53. *Comeback America* by The Hon. David M. Walker

54. *The Science of getting rich* by Wallace D. Wattles

55. *Personal Benchmark* by Chuck Widger and Dr. Daniel Crosby

56. *Bank on Yourself* by Pamela Yellen

About the Author

Vijay Khetarpal, AIF®, CLU®, ChFC®, CFP®
President & CEO
Integrity Financial Group, LLC
Tysons Corner, Virginia
www.integrityfinancial.com

Vijay Khetarpal has been dedicated to providing exceptional service and financial advice to his clients since 1983. Holder of a degree in Economics, with honors, from St. Stephens College at Delhi University, India, Vijay has continued his career-related education and has earned the professional designations of Accredited Investment Fiduciary (AIF®), Chartered Life Underwriter(CLU®), Chartered Financial Consultant (ChFC®) and Certified Financial Planner(CFP®).

Vijay is President and Chief Executive Officer of Integrity Financial Group, LLC, located in Tyson's Corner, Virginia. He describes his work as helping to create, protect, and preserve wealth with the motto, "We help protect your tomorrows." His areas of concentration are employee benefits, estate planning, retirement planning, and life insurance for a clientele composed largely of successful professionals and corporations, with a special focus on companies employing up to 500 employees, especially in the high-tech sector.

"In serving my clients," Vijay says, "I shall recommend that course of action which I would apply to myself in the same situation. I see myself as an extension of the Human Resource department for my corporate clients. And a financial quarterback if you may for my individual clients."

Vijay is the recipient of many industry honors, including the National Quality Award (NQA) and membership in the Million Dollar

Round Table (MDRT) and Top of the Table. He also is a member of Forum 400. In addition, he is a member of the National Association of Insurance and Financial Advisors (NAIFA), the Financial Planning Association (FPA), and the Society of Financial Service Professionals (SFSP). He has been listed in *Who's Who in Finance*, and he has contributed articles to regional and industry publications. In 2017 he founded the Capital Area Professional Advisors Roundtable (CAPART) which is a Study group and Think tank of Professional Advisors in Allied professions.

Vijay often gives seminars and has appeared on local community television programs. In addition, he is a past president of the local chapter of his professional association, and he is a past president of the Rotary Club of Potomac, Maryland.

In his leisure time, Vijay enjoys sports, especially the games of squash, golf, and skiing, and he enjoys watching NFL games. In addition, he is fond of travel, reading, music, and fine dining. Mostly, he enjoys spending time with his wife, Anila; and their beautifully blended family of three boys, Vikram, Andy, and Vinay, their wives; and grandchildren.

If you have any comments, feedback, questions or business inquiries, please send an email to **vijay@integrityfinancial.com**.

Endnotes

1. To learn more about Mayo College, Ajmer, visit https://mayocollege.com/.

2. Indices are unmanaged, and investors cannot invest directly in an index.

3. The Standard & Poor's 500 (S&P 500) is an unmanaged group of securities considered to be representative of the stock market in general. It is a market-value-weighted index with each stock's weight in the index proportionate to its market value.

4. **Please consider the investment objectives, risks, charges, expenses, and your need for death-benefit coverage carefully before investing. The prospectus, which contains this and other information about the variable life policy and the underlying investment options, can be obtained from your financial professional. Be sure to read the prospectus carefully before deciding whether to invest.**

   The investment return and principal value of the variable life policy are not guaranteed. Variable life sub-accounts fluctuate with changes in market conditions. The principal may be worth more or less than the original amount invested when the policy is surrendered. Any guarantees offered are backed by the financial strength of the insurance company.

5. Indexed universal life insurance is an insurance contract that, depending on the contract, may offer a guaranteed annual interest rate and some participation growth, if any, of a stock market index. Such contracts have substantial variation in terms, costs of guarantees, and features and may cap participation or returns in significant ways. Any guarantees offered are backed by the financial strength of the insurance company, not an outside entity. Investors are cautioned to carefully review an indexed universal life insurance for its features, costs, risks, and how the variables are calculated.

6. Riders are available for an additional fee—some riders may not be available in all states.

7. "Walt Disney Timeline," JustDisney.com, http://www.justdisney.com/walt_disney/timeline/nextpage.html.

8. "Famous People Who Used the Bank on Yourself Method," Bank on Yourself, https://www.bankonyourself.com/famous-people-who-use-the-bank-on-yourself-method.html.

9. The Technical and Miscellaneous Revenue Act (TAMRA) that was signed into law on November 10, 1988, alters the tax treatment of distributions from certain types of life insurance policies. The law applies to all policies issued or materially changed on or after June 21, 1988.

   If premiums paid on such a policy are in excess of the limits established by Congress, then the policy is classified as a Modified Endowment Contract (MEC). If there is a gain in the contract, the portion of the gain included in any distribution, including policy loans, will be reported as taxable income. If a distribution occurs prior to the insured attaining 59½, the taxable portion of the distribution may also be subject to a 10 percent tax penalty.

A policy that, at issue is, or later becomes Modified Endowment Contract will always be subject to MEC tax treatment. This applies even if the policy is exchanged for a new contract that, standing alone, would not be a MEC. Tax-deferred growth in cash values and tax-free death benefits are still available under a MEC.

10. "Modified Endowment Contract (MEC,) Akhilesh Ganti, Investopedia, updated September 13, 2019. https://www.investopedia.com/terms/m/modified-endowment-contract.asp.

11. Ibid.

12. Diversification does not guarantee a profit or protect against a loss in a declining market. It is a method used to help manage investment risk.

13. Rebalancing/reallocating can entail transaction costs and tax consequences that should be considered when determining a rebalancing/reallocation strategy.

14. Investing in alternative assets involves higher risks than traditional investments and is suitable only for sophisticated investors. Alternative investments are often sold by prospectus that discloses all risks, fees, and expenses. They are not tax-efficient, and an investor should consult with his/her tax advisor prior to investing. Alternative investments have higher fees than traditional investments, and they may also be highly leveraged and engage in speculative investment techniques, which can magnify the potential for investment loss or gain and should not be deemed a complete investment program. The value of the investment may fall as well as rise, and investors may get back less than they invested.

15. "The sector Investing Opportunity," Fidelity Investments, May 2015, http://strategic-financial-planning.com/files/Sector_Specialist_Presentation_07.27.15.pdf.

16. Asset allocation does not guarantee a profit or protect against a loss in a declining market. t is a method used to help manage investment risk.

17. "Equities: The Basics," Amelia Josephson, January 21, 2020, Smart Asset™, https://smartasset.com/investing/what-are-equities.

18. **Mutual funds and exchange traded funds (ETFs) are sold by prospectus. Please consider the investment objectives, risks, charges, and expenses carefully before investing. The prospectus, which contains this and other information about the investment company, can be obtained from the Fund Company or your financial professional. Be sure to read the prospectus carefully before deciding whether to invest.**

19. Investments in emerging markets may be more volatile and less liquid than investing in developed markets and may involve exposure to economic structures that are generally less diverse and mature and to political systems that have less stability than those of more developed countries.

20. Investments in commodities may have greater volatility than investments in traditional securities, particularly if the instruments involve leverage. The value of commodity-linked derivative instruments may be affected by changes in overall market movements, commodity index volatility, changes in interest rates, or factors affecting a particular industry or commodity, such as drought, floods, weather, livestock disease, embargoes, tariffs, and international economic,

21. Dollar cost averaging may help reduce per share cost through continuous investment in securities, regardless of fluctuating prices, and does not guarantee profitability nor can it protect from loss in a declining market. The investor should consider his/her ability to continue investing through periods of low price levels.

22. "Dollar-Cost Averaging (DCA)," James Chen, Investopedia, updated on March 16, 2020, https://www.investopedia.com/terms/d/dollarcostaveraging.asp.

23. Bradford Tax Institute, "History of Federal Income Tax Rates: 1913–2020. https://bradfordtaxinstitute.com/Free_Resources/Federal-Income-Tax-Rates.aspx.

24. Pursuant to requirements imposed by the Internal Revenue Service, any tax advice contained in this communication (including any attachments) is not intended to be used, and cannot be used, for purposes of avoiding penalties imposed under the United States Internal Revenue Code or promoting, marketing, or recommending to another person any tax-related matter. Please contact us if you wish to have formal written advice on this matter.

25. "Estate Tax," Julia Kagan, Investopedia, updated July 22, 2019, https://www.investopedia.com/terms/e/estatetax.asp.

26. "A Will That Cooked Up a Tangled Web," Sharon Walsh, Los Angeles Times, August 3, 1997, https://www.latimes.com/archives/la-xpm-1997-aug-03-sp-18984-story.html.

27. "Irrevocable Trust," Bankrate, https://www.bankrate.com/glossary/i/irrevocable-trust/.

28. Ibid.

29. "Retirement Plan and IRA Required Minimum Distributions FAQs," the Internal Revenue Service, https://www.irs.gov/retirement-plans/retirement-plans-faqs-regarding-required-minimum-distributions.

30. "Coronavirus Aid, Relief, and Economic Security (CARES) Act," Jim Chappelow, Investopedia, updated June 23, 2020, https://www.investopedia.com/coronavirus-aid-relief-and-economic-security-cares-act-4800707.

31. Fixed annuities are long-term insurance contacts, and there is a surrender charge imposed generally during the first 5 to 7 years that you own the annuity contract. Withdrawals prior to age 59½ may result in a 10 percent IRS tax penalty, in addition to any ordinary income tax. Any guarantees of the annuity are backed by the financial strength of the underlying insurance company.

32. "The Secret to a Happier Retirement: Friends, Neighbors and a Fixed Annuity," Jonathan Clements, The Wall Street Journal, updated July 27, 2005, https://www.wsj.com/articles/SB112241804795796704.

33. "Life Expectancy and Mortality Rates in the United States, 1957–2017," Steven H. Woolf, MD, MPH, and Heidi Schoomaker, MAEd, JAMA Network, November 26, 2019, https://jamanetwork.com/journals/jama/article-abstract/2756187?guestAccessKey=c1202c42-e6b9-4c99-a936-0976a270551f&utm_source=For_The_Media&utm_medium=referral&utm_campaign=ftm_links&utm_content=tfl&utm_term=112619.

34. "The Most Popular Ages to Collect Social Security," Emily Brandon, US News & World Report, January 22, 2020, https://money.usnews.com/money/retirement/social-security/articles/the-most-popular-ages-to-collect-social-security.

35. "Working Later in Life Can Pay Off in More than Just Income," Harvard Medical School's Harvard Health Letter, June 2018, https://www.health.harvard.edu/staying-healthy/working-later-in-life-can-pay-off-in-more-than-just-income.

36. "HR 1994—Setting Every Community Up for Retirement Enhancement Act of 2019," Congress.gov, https://www.congress.gov/bill/116th-congress/house-bill/1994?q=%7B%22search%22%3A%5B%22Setting+Every+Community+Up+for+Retirement+Enhancement+Act%22%5D%7D&s=2&r=1.

37. "What Is the SECURE Act and How Could It Affect Your Retirement?" Daniel Kurt, Investopedia, updated January 20, 2020, https://www.investopedia.com/what-is-secure-act-how-affect-retirement-4692743.

38. "Cornelius Vanderbilt," History.com, updated September 9, 2019, https://www.history.com/topics/19th-century/cornelius-vanderbilt.

39. "The Vanderbilts: How American Royalty Lost Their Crown Jewels," Natalie Robehmed, Forbes, July 14, 2014, https://www.forbes.com/sites/natalierobehmed/2014/07/14/the-vanderbilts-how-american-royalty-lost-their-crown-jewels/#1b3b743f353b.

40. Ibid.

41. "America's Oldest Billion-Dollar Family Fortunes," Katia Savchuk, Forbes, July 1, 2015, https://www.forbes.com/sites/katiasavchuk/2015/07/01/americas-oldest-billion-dollar-family-fortunes/#63a0857e240f.

42. "How to Create a Family Bank?" Laura Pitko, YouTube video, June 29, 2019, https://www.youtube.com/watch?v=DsTnuoAXMNk.

43. "Closely Held Corporations," Encyclopedia of Business, 2nd edition, https://www.referenceforbusiness.com/encyclopedia/Clo-Con/Closely-Held-Corporations.html.

44. "Capital Gains Tax," Julia Kagan, Investopedia, updated June 25, 2019, https://www.investopedia.com/terms/c/capital_gains_tax.asp.

45. Split-dollar insurance is not an insurance policy; it is a method of paying for insurance coverage. A split-dollar plan is an arrangement between two parties that involves "splitting" the premium payments, cash values, ownership of the policy, and death benefits. These arrangements are subject to Split Dollar Final Regulations that apply for purposes of federal income, employment, and gift taxes. Regulations provide that the tax treatment of split-dollar life insurance arrangements will be determined under one of two sets of rules, depending on who owns the policy.

46. "How Cash Value Life Insurance Made Jim Harbaugh a Top-Paid Coach," Jordan Smith, JD, LLM, Schechter, October 4, 2017, https://www.schechterwealth.com/2017/10/04/cash-value-life-insurance-jim-harbaugh/.

47. Ibid.

48. Ibid.

49. "7 Things You Need to Know About 409A Valuation," Larry Kim, Inc., May 31, 2017, https://www.inc.com/larry-kim/7-things-you-need-to-know-about-409a-valuation.html.

50. "The New Golden Handcuffs," Stephen O. Kroeger, Jack F. Elder, and Ryan Mattern, InsuranceNewsNet magazine, September 2012, p. 38.

51. Ibid.

52. 75 Percent of Americans Are Winging It when It Comes to Their Financial Future, Jessica Dickler, CNBC, April 2, 2019, https://www.cnbc.com/2019/04/01/when-it-comes-to-their-financial-future-most-americans-are-winging-it.html.

www.ingramcontent.com/pod-product-compliance
Lightning Source LLC
Chambersburg PA
CBHW061259120726
48001CB00001B/373

* 9 7 9 8 6 9 4 9 5 4 6 1 7 *